STARTING FRESH!

While every effort has been made to verify the accuracy of material included in this book, neither the author nor the publisher can assume any responsibility for errors.

Book Design: Leslie Rindoks
Photography, unless otherwise noted © Kurt Rindoks
Produce photo, page x by Jill Dahan
Pomegranate, page 112 by Lifdig

ISBN: 978-0-9838936-7-7
Library of Congress: 2013939760

AUTHOR'S ACKNOWLEDGEMENTS

First of all, I would like to thank everyone that took part in making this book a reality. It has been an adventure that I couldn't have made without every single one of you!

I would also like to thank:

Leslie for all her creativity and vision. This book would not have existed without her;

Kurt for going out on a limb but transforming this book with his photos;

Cassie and Karen for all their tasting and schlepping;

my men at home (plus Frankie) who are my harshest critics, but also my constant encouragement;

and to my dear friend Sally in the UK who, with the original cooking school bunch, inspired the journey that led me to my true passion in life.

STARTING FRESH!

RECIPES FOR LIFE
by Jill Dahan

We are indeed
MUCH MORE THAN
WHAT WE EAT
—*but*—
WHAT WE EAT,
can nevertheless
help us to be

MUCH MORE THAN
WHAT WE ARE.

—*Alice May Brock*

No matter how busy our lives are, cooking and eating nutritiously is something we can all do.

MY RECIPE FOR LIFE:
Combine fresh food, great taste, and love.

[contents]

BREAKFAST

SAVORY SNACKS

SALADS & SOUPS

VEGGIE SIDES

VEGGIE MAINS

SEAFOOD

MEAT

SWEETS

[getting started]

First, thank you for buying this book! Whether you are a seasoned cook, or one who rarely turns on the oven, you'll be amazed at how easy it is to make a fresh start and enjoy better health and wellbeing. There is no magic or rocket science to making delicious dishes packed with nutrition. All it takes is a bit of planning, a tad more time, and a good sense of adventure!

My love affair with cooking began when I knew next to nothing about food. Believe it or not, there was a time when my friends didn't think I could make anything that didn't come out of a box! Exposure to different cultures and foods while living and working in London marked the start of my culinary adventure. I later travelled across Europe, to the Middle East, and then Australia and New Zealand, gaining lifelong friends along the way. While travelling, I made a point to visit farm stands and local markets. My cooking evolved from "what I knew" to "what was new to me."

Eventually I landed in the quaint English village of Sunninghill where I raised three boys and began teaching cooking classes. At first I relied on familiar family recipes; as I gathered confidence I created my own recipes, incorporating new ideas and ingredients.

As with most things, the first step is to get organized. So go ahead and spend a few minutes straightening your pantry. Then wander through this book and select a handful of recipes to build a week's menu. Make your shopping list—the following Kitchen Primer will help you get started—and you'll be on your way!

LIFE CHANGING

I am not a doctor or a trained chef; I can't make medical claims or dazzle you with my knife skills — but I am a wife and a mother of three growing boys and I strive to nourish my family in the best way possible. Like many, we have struggled with acne, weight issues, high blood pressure, high cholesterol and cancer. When I began to educate myself about nutrition, I realized the transformative power of food.

After my family and I moved to the States a few years ago, I baked everything from scratch so my kids wouldn't get used to the sweeter taste found in many American foods. Even though my boys begged, "Please, no more homemade stuff. Can't we just have store bought like everyone else?" I ignored them. And while my sons clamored for store-bought treats, I noticed their friends gobbled up everything I made.

> "The most important and most powerful tool you have to change your health is your fork."
> —Dr. Mark Hyman

When my oldest son developed cystic acne we were advised it could be helped only with powerful drugs. We opted for a different approach and attempted a cure by changing what he ate, specifically eliminating dairy and processed sugars. I devised a cookie recipe that was not only healthy, but gave him energy while satisfying his sweet tooth. Others tasted these cookies, loved them, and "Jill's Hills" were born. Soon Sunninghill Jill's Baking Business was supplying two national supermarkets as well as local cafés. My son's acne improved dramatically (and so did his grades). Life was good!

Then one August afternoon, another of my sons was injured playing football. Treatment in the Emergency Room led to the discovery that he had a very rare form of cancer. Shock, terror, disbelief and helplessness engulfed me. After his first surgery, I felt strongly that diet would make a difference and I went into overdrive educating myself about food and nutrition. I scoured every anti-cancer and health book I could lay my hands on. Real food, lots of veggies, and low sugar were the main themes in everything I read. So I rolled up my sleeves and took to my kitchen where I created dish after dish in efforts to nurse him back to health. Ingredients I had relied on for years

were no longer an option. I searched for nutritionally better—and hopefully tastier—alternatives. I had a lot of flops but eventually achieved some success.

> Each meal is a chance to heal.

The more I learned the more I realized this wasn't just for my son, it was for all of us. I felt better—more clear-headed—after changing my eating habits. My husband's blood pressure, weight and cholesterol improved as well. Cancer, however, is unpredictable; and while I don't know what the future holds, I do know that we ultimately are much more healthy than we've ever been.

COLORFUL AND DELICIOUS

I am determined to dispel the myth that healthy food tastes bland. Healthy food is not the health food you may remember from the "weird and wonderful" aisle in the grocery store where everything was brown.

Explore your grocer's produce section or even better, a farmers' market. Drink in the incredible variety of color and texture, smell the fragrant herbs, sample something you may never have tried before.

And learn as much as you can about the food you choose to eat.

I have enjoyed getting to know many of my local growers, like the mushroom guru who supplements his farmers' market income with marriage counselling. (Or maybe it's the other way around.) There is a family who has the most spectacular eggs—beautiful pale blues, almost too good looking to crack open! They're one of my first stops as they sell out within 30 minutes of the market opening. The sprout man, too, is an early visit; he sits quietly and sells out quickly.

Not so long ago we all ate local, organic food. Most meals were eaten at home. There were no fast-food restaurants, there was no junk food—there was just what your mother or grandmother made. Choosing fresh foods from your local farmers' market, your backyard garden, and the produce section of your local grocery are the first steps to waging a nourishing revolution.

EMBRACE THE NEW

Fresh is best, but if fresh isn't available, use frozen. Just try to avoid processed products. As you readjust your taste buds, you'll begin to taste the *food* rather than the sugar and salt that are the predominant flavors in processed foods.

Nutritionally dense foods fuel your brain and your body. Consuming fresh foods — without the addition of sugar, hydrogenated fats, additives, and food dyes — will help you feel better, look better, and think more clearly.

Because I no longer rely on adding refined sugar or salt to a dish to make it more appealing, I have become more creative. I am using products I never knew existed, or using them in unexpected ways to achieve that "wow" factor while delivering the most nutritious bang possible. (My kids say I try to eke out every healthy twist I can in a dish and they are right.) I sleep better knowing I am nourishing my family – not just feeding them.

Some ingredients in this book may be new to you. Others you may use in ways you never imagined. (You may not want to disclose every ingredient before your family tries a taste.)

One of the most radical changes I propose is making coconut oil your main cooking oil. Use virgin coconut oil—unbleached, non-hydrogenated, unrefined, and unfermented. (Cold pressed is great!)

In the 1960s, coconut oil was erroneously labeled as unhealthy. Studies claimed tropical coconut oils were laden with artery-clogging fats. However, the coconut oil used in the studies was hydrogenated – not *virgin* coconut oil used for centuries as a staple food. We now know the real culprit is hydrogenation—artificially adding a hydrogen molecule to oils in order to make the oil shelf-stable. All hydrogenated oils—

Why COCONUT oil?

soy, corn, and canola—contain dangerous trans-fats and are processed with toxic hexane solvents.

Better than butter in all types of baking and cooking, coconut oil has a light taste and pleasant aroma. (Adding a pinch of sea salt further reduces the subtle coconut flavor.) Unlike olive oil, it does not break down into free radicals when heated. You can store coconut oil at room temperature; it is solid up to 76°F before it melts.

This brain food contains no cholesterol or sodium and has actually shown to help memory function. Coconuts are one of the few foods that contain rare nutrients known as medium chain fatty acids (MCFAs). Additional health benefits include: improved digestion, improved metabolism, and greater stability with blood sugar levels. Used topically, it also soothes eczema, psoriasis, and conditions dry hair.

Additionally, I suggest you replace refined sugar with coconut sugar. Coconut sugar is minimally processed, unbleached and contains no preservatives. Coconut sugar is made from the nectar of coconut flower blossoms and is especially high in minerals including zinc, potassium, calcium, nitrogen, and magnesium as well as vitamins B2, B3, and B6 and has 16 vital amino acids. With its caramel undertones, it is tastier than refined sugar. Another nice benefit: you can use half to two thirds as much as regular cane or brown sugar to achieve the sweet balance desserts deserve.

In this book, I have combined everything I have learned about foods, flavors, and nutrition to create mouthwatering dishes that nourish the body and delight the taste buds. I have tested these recipes on pretty picky eaters — kids, teenagers and adults. No one has walked away from my table hungry. In fact, they often ask for seconds, or for the recipe!

[*"There are no great acts; only small acts done with great love."* —Mother Teresa]

Roll up your sleeves and get cooking! Start creating your own small acts with love—for yourself, your family, and your friends!

~Jill Dahan

kitchen PRIMER

Even though I've cooked in million dollar kitchens with all the bells and whistles and baked cookies for crowned princes, I've also made do in dorm rooms with only a microwave. I have fed hordes of hungry hikers with nothing more than a camp stove. A well-equipped kitchen doesn't require that many items. Here's a list of what I consider the basics:

good, strong blender
a few good knives
measuring spoons
slotted spoon
silicone spatula
whisk
vegetable peeler
garlic press
cheese grater
fine mesh strainer
dry and liquid measuring cups
1 small frying pan
1 large frying pan
1 medium sauce pan
1 roasting pan
pyrex baking dishes, 8x8 and 9x13
spring form pan, 8- or 9-inch
cupcake pans, regular and mini
baking sheet
heavy casserole dish with lid (Dutch oven)

[ingredients to keep on hand]

almonds, blanched whole These nuts are one of oldest healing foods in the world. They are rich in protein, fiber, calcium, vitamin E and magnesium. They are also "blood sugar friendly" as they contain no carbs. Those who consume more nuts typically have lower body mass indexes.

almond butter, unsweetened

almond flour You can buy this pre-ground or, for half the cost, make your own using a blender. Roughly ⅔ - ¾ cup of whole blanched almonds makes 1 cup ground almond flour.

almond milk, unsweetened

balsamic vinegar

baking powder, aluminum-free

butter (unsalted, organic is best)

coconut oil I use Nutiva. It's available online and in certain grocery stores. (See page xi for more on the benefits of coconut oil.)

coconut milk This can be used instead of dairy or almond milk; it adds a subtle sweetness to recipes. It is sold in cans in the baking aisle.

coconut sugar (See page xi.)

dates Buy the type with stones intact as they stay moister.

dark chocolate, 70% or above Cocoa solids not only boost serotonin which improves mood, but they also reduce the risk of heart attack and stroke because they contain magnesium, shown to lower blood pressure. Stick to dark chocolate (not milk or white) and avoid chocolate loaded with sugar, waxes, fats and chemicals. Cocoa butter (a good fat) is not hydrogenated.

Dijon mustard

eggs large, organic (pasture raised if possible)

filo dough (I prefer Filo Factory brand) Use whole wheat if you can find it.

fresh lemons and limes

fresh onions, red and yellow

frozen fruit Keep mango, blueberries, raspberries, pineapple, and strawberries in your freezer.

goat cheese This cheese has more digestible fat and protein than traditional dairy cheese and is naturally lactose free. Goat cheese has more calcium, magnesium, potassium and vitamin A than cow-based cheese, though less B12 and folic acid.

Greek yogurt Greek yogurt is full of protein. Go for low fat or full fat as the calcium is better absorbed with fat and you will feel fuller longer!

herbs, such as: basil, mint, rosemary, thyme

honey Raw and unfiltered is best.

jam, all fruit, no sugar added I love St. Dalfour and if you have a Trader Joe's nearby, try their organic Super Fruit Fruit Spread.

maple syrup, grade B This type contains more calcium and nutrients than other grades.

olive oil, extra virgin Olive oil has been shown to lower blood pressure and decrease the risk of colon and bowel cancer. However, do not heat olive oil! High heat damages its flavor and negates its health benefits. When exposed to high heat, olive oil breaks down into free radicals. Grill veggies first, then toss in olive oil. Likewise, bake croutons, then brush with oil, garlic and herbs.

parmesan cheese Regianno is the tastiest.

pasta Try DeBoule's pasta, made from artichoke flour for a delicous alternative to bland-tasting pastas.

puff pastry I prefer Trader Joe's or Dufour brands. All butter puff pastry is best.

quinoa Be sure to try red and black types, too!

salsa I am a big fan of Amy's Salsa!

sea salt I prefer Maldon.

spices, such as: chili flakes, cinnamon, cumin seeds, curry powder, ginger, and oregano

spinach and other fresh greens

Tahini (ground sesame seed paste)

tomato paste Salt-free is best and bottled tastes better than canned.

tomatoes, whole or crushed For best taste, look for bottled rather than canned.

vanilla bean paste Use this instead of vanilla extract to really elevate your baking. Because it contains no alcohol, it won't dilute your dish—it gently thickens instead. (I use Nielsen-Massey.)

walnuts, raw and unsalted

NOTE: While some of these ingredients are more costly than the alternatives you may be accustomed to using, in most instances, the items will pay for themselves.

- *It takes smaller quantities of nutrient dense food to satisfy even the most demanding appetites, so you will need less.*
- *You will be spending less on packaged goods. Why pay for cardboard and plastic, when you can put your money toward tastier, fresher and healthier food?*

breakfast

EGGS

Loaded with vitamins, minerals and protein, eggs are one of nature's most perfect foods. Relatively inexpensive, they can be prepared in a zillion ways.

Eggs, having all eight essential amino acids, are beneficial for cardiovascular and brain health. The choline found in egg yolks helps prevent the collection of cholesterol and fat in the liver. Choline also boosts the brain's memory power for 4-5 hours after eating.

Organic eggs are higher in omega-3s which are are extremely beneficial in preventing heart disease. (Buy pasture-raised if you can.)

Breakfast on the Fly

[Serves 1]

½ tsp coconut oil or butter for greasing ramekin
1 slice tomato
a few fresh baby spinach leaves
1 large egg
1 tbsp unsweetened almond or cows milk
1 tbsp feta, cheddar, or goat cheese, crumbled

Brush a little oil inside a small ramekin and then put tomato slice on the bottom. Microwave for 20 seconds. Add spinach, egg, milk, and sprinkle with cheese. Microwave for 30 seconds for soft yolk or a little longer for harder yolk.

Alternatively: Bake in the oven for 5 minutes with the tomato in the ramekin and then add the rest of the ingredients as above and bake 4-5 minutes for runny eggs or 6-7 minutes for harder yolks.

Egg Wrap with Summer Veggies

[Serves 4]

4 large eggs
1 tbsp fresh thyme, basil or tarragon
coconut oil or melted butter for coating the pan

OPTIONAL FILLINGS
about 1 cup (4 oz) (115g) sautéed veggies (zucchini, tomato, leeks, onion, avocado, mushroom, spinach, etc)
½ cup (2 oz) (55g) mild goat cheese, feta, or other cheese
salsa

Beat eggs until frothy and add herbs.

Heat a small, nonstick pan then coat with oil or butter. Turn heat to low and pour in ¼ of the mixture. Swirl to cover the bottom of the pan. Cook 2 minutes until set then carefully slide onto a plate.

Place about ¼ cup sautéed veggies and a sprinkling of cheese down the center and fold both sides in to cover. Keep warm and repeat with remaining mixture to make three additional wraps. Serve warm with salsa.

Frittata

[Serves 6]

12 large eggs
6 tbsp water
8 oz log (about 2 cups) (225g) mild goat cheese
3 tbsp fresh thyme or oregano leaves
1 tsp coconut oil for pan
3 cups (5 oz) (145g) fresh baby spinach
½ red onion, sliced
1 red pepper, sliced and deseeded
½ cup (4oz) (115g) sundried tomatoes, diced
½ cup (2 oz) (55g) parmesan, grated

Place eggs, water, thyme, and half the goat cheese log in a blender and blend until combined. Coat roasting pan with a little oil and add the red pepper and onion slices. Bake at 375°F (190°C) for about 10-15 minutes, until softened. Remove from the oven and add the spinach and tomatoes and toss to wilt spinach.

Grease a 9-inch removeable bottom pan and heat in a 375°F (190°C) oven for 3 minutes. Add the egg mixture and top with the sautéed veggies. Bake for 18-20 minutes until just set, then top with the rest of the goat cheese and parmesan. Heat 3 minutes to melt. Serve in wedges.

This recipe can be done in muffin cups for individual portions; just reduce the cooking time to 10-13 minutes until set.

4

Raspberry Lime Loaves

[Makes 1 loaf]

1 cup (8 oz) (22g) unsalted butter
or ¾ cup (6 oz) (170g) coconut oil
½ cup (2½ oz) (70g) coconut sugar
4 large eggs
2 tsp baking powder
1½ cups (6 oz) (170g) whole wheat or
sprouted wheat flour
¾ cup (3 oz) (85g) blanched almond flour*
juice of 1 lime
¼ cup (2 oz) (55ml) coconut milk
1 cup (5 oz) (145g) fresh or frozen raspberries

Beat butter or oil and sugar until creamed. Add eggs and 1 tbsp flour and beat until light and creamy.

In a separate bowl, combine baking powder with the flour and almond flour. Fold into the egg mixture.

Grease 1 loaf pan. Fill pan three-quarters full and top with raspberries. Bake at 375°F (190°C) for 25-30 minutes until toothpick comes out with just crumbs on it.

*To make your own almond flour, grind about ¾ cup of whole blanched almonds in a blender to make 1 cup almond flour. Excess almond flour can be stored in the freezer for future use.

Blueberry Muffins

Here are some muffins worth waking up for!

[Makes 9-10 muffins]

2 large eggs
6 tbsp extra virgin coconut oil
2 tsp vanilla bean paste
⅔ cup (5 fl oz) (70ml) unsweetened almond or dairy milk
6 tbsp coconut sugar
2 cups (8 oz) (225g) whole wheat or sprouted wheat flour*
2 tsp baking powder
1 cup (5 oz) (145g) fresh or frozen blueberries

Bring all ingredients to room temperature. Blend eggs, oil, vanilla, and milk until thoroughly combined. Set aside.

In a mixing bowl, combine sugar, flour, and baking powder. Add liquid ingredients to the dry mixture, mixing only until combined. Batter may be lumpy. Stir in blueberries.

Line muffin tins and split mixture evenly. (Fill any empty muffin cups halfway with water to ensure even baking.) Bake at 375°F (190°C) for about 18 minutes until lightly browned and toothpick comes out with just crumbs attached.

*GLUTEN FREE OPTION: instead of whole wheat flour, substitute 1 cup (4 oz) (115g) old fashioned oats, plus ¾ cup (4 oz) (115g) whole, blanched almonds. Grind together in blender until fine as flour.

Banana Muffins

Great when your bananas have turned a little black or were reduced at the market. (If your bananas have gotten too ripe, but you can't make these straight away, just pop them in the freezer.) These muffins are great for breakfast, in lunchboxes, or as afternoon snacks. Plus this recipe is gluten free and protein rich thanks to the oats, almonds and yogurt..

[Makes 12]

1 cup (4 oz) (115g) old fashioned oats
1 cup (4 oz) (115g) blanched almond flour*
1 tsp baking powder
3 very ripe bananas
½ cup (4 oz) (115g) plain Greek yogurt
2 tsp vanilla bean paste
⅓ cup (2½ oz) (75g) extra virgin coconut oil
2 large eggs
3 pitted dates

dark chocolate mini chunks (optional)

Place oats in blender; blend on high until flour-like consistency. Transfer to mixing bowl and add baking powder and almond flour. Then blend bananas, yogurt, vanilla, oil, eggs and dates until smooth. Mix liquid ingredients with dry and stir in chocolate if using. Spoon mixture into a prepared muffin tins. (Fill any empty muffin cups halfway with water to ensure even baking.)

Bake at 375°F (190°C) for about 18-20 minutes, until lightly browned on top and toothpick comes out with just crumbs.

To make your own almond flour, simply grind about ¾ cup of whole blanched almonds in a blender to make 1 cup almond flour.

Quickie Oatmeal

This is a very creamy "like you get at nice hotel breakfasts" porridge. Soaking packs an extra nutritious boost and is key to quick cooking. Be brave and try this oatmeal with almond milk. It adds a subtle sweetness and a little extra nuttiness. Kids think it tastes great!

[Serves 2]

1 (4 oz) (115g) cup old fashioned oats
2-3 cups (16-24 fl oz) (500ml-750ml) unsweetened almond or dairy milk

OPTIONAL TOPPINGS:
honey, maple syrup,
raisins, date pieces, walnuts, almonds,
fresh fruit

Soak oats overnight by placing them in a bowl and covering with at least 2 inches of water.

In the morning, drain the water and then pour enough milk over the oats to cover. Bring to a boil on the stovetop. Then cover, reducing heat to low. Simmer 5 minutes, adding more milk to desired consistency.

Remove from heat. If porridge is too thick, add a little more milk. Serve with toppings, if desired.

Oaty Bars

These are a staple in my house during school term times. They are great for breakfast on the go, lunchtime treat, after school snack, or late night study break. You can add in dark chocolate chips if that is your thing but try them without as they are yummy sans chocolate.

[Makes 9-12 bars]

⅓ cup (2½ oz) (75g) extra virgin coconut oil or unsalted butter
2 tbsp unsalted almond butter, (smooth or crunchy)
¼ cup (1¼ oz) (35g) coconut sugar
1½ cups (6 oz) (175g) old fashioned oats, ground finely in a blender
¼ cup (1 oz) (28g) unsalted raw sunflower seeds, ground finely

Melt oil or butter and mix with almond butter and sugar until combined. Add oats and seeds and stir until coated.

Grease a glass or light colored pan (8x8) with butter or oil and press mixture firmly in the bottom.

Bake on the middle rack in the oven at 350°F (180°C) for 20 minutes until lightly browned. Remove, press mixture down with spatula again and cool in fridge or freezer. Cut into squares when completely cool.

(Dark chocolate chips can be added for a special treat.)

Homemade Granola

You will never want to buy premade granola again! Make a bunch and store in the freezer to have at the ready for toppings on fruit, ice cream, yogurt, oatmeal, fresh fruit crumble, or just plain munching! Go crazy and use whatever you have on hand. Try mixing and matching with walnuts, cashews, pistachios, pecans, or macadamia nuts.

[Serves 4]

3 tbsp extra virgin coconut oil or unsalted butter
2 tbsp raw honey
2 cups (8 oz) (225g) old fashioned oats
½ cup (2 oz) (55g) raw unsalted slivered almonds
½ (2 oz) (55g) cup raw unsalted sunflower seeds
½ cup (2 oz) (55g) raisins and or dried fruit (optional)

Heat the oil or butter and honey in a pan until warm. Add oats, nuts, and seeds and stir until combined. Spread the mixture thinly on a nonstick roasting pan or baking sheet and place in the oven on the middle rack at 325° F (170°C) for 20-25 minutes until lightly browned. Check and toss half way through. Remove and add raisins and or dried fruit and let cool.

Raspberry Greek Yogurt

1 cup (5 oz) (145g) raspberries (fresh or frozen)
3-4 tbsp all fruit raspberry jam (I use St Dalfour)
2 cups (16 oz) (450g) plain Greek yogurt

Swirl jam into yogurt, and layer in dishes with fruit and granola.

BERRIES

Fresh, frozen, or dried, berries are nutritional powerhouses. They enhance memory function and help prevent urinary tract infections. Berries are also naturally high in antioxidants — compounds that enhance immune function, protect cells from damage from free radicals, and possibly inhibit cell mutations that result in abnormal growths.

Blueberries are repeatedly ranked as having one of the highest antioxidant capacities among all fruits and vegetables. Blueberries help memory, motor skills, balance and coordination. In addition, they help arteries contract (good for blood pressure) and have been shown to reduce stroke damage. The white, powdery substance on blueberries called "bloom" indicates the berries' freshness and is a protective coating, so only wash blueberries just before serving.

Raspberries are a member of the rose family and come in other colors besides red. They contain bone-building vitamin K and are the highest source of ellagic acid which offers powerful cancer-fighting benefits.

Strawberries, while technically not a berry, nonetheless abound with healthy benefits. Eight strawberries provide 160% of the daily recommended amount of vitamin C.

Waffles

[Makes 4-5 waffles]

2 large eggs
⅓ cup (2½ oz) (70g) extra virgin coconut oil or melted butter
½ cup (4 oz) (125g) plain Greek yogurt
½ cup (4 fl oz) (125ml) unsweetened almond or dairy milk
1 cup (4 oz) (115g) whole wheat or sprouted wheat flour
1 tsp baking powder

Preheat waffle iron. Blend (in a blender or by hand): eggs, oil, yogurt, and milk. Add flour and baking powder and mix just until combined. Pour about ⅓ cup of mixture into each waffle iron imprint and cook 3 minutes for softer waffles or 5 minutes for crunchy waffles. Top with fruit or syrup.

For a savory waffle, top with egg and cheese.

Fresh Fruit Sauce

1 cup (5 oz) (145g) fresh (or frozen and defrosted) strawberries
2-3 tbsp all fruit strawberry jam (I use St Dalfour)

Blend fruit with jam and warm slightly to serve.

French Toast with Benefits

A nutritionist once recommended Ezekiel bread as a great alternative to whole wheat or white bread. Since then, I've experimented with this healthful alternative to discover recipes that even my children love. Voilá! Here is a winner.

[Serves 2-3]

6 slices whole wheat or Ezekiel bread (I use cinnamon raisin)
4 large eggs
cinnamon for sprinkling (optional)
pure maple syrup or fresh fruit sauce for serving (see below)
1 tbsp extra virgin coconut oil or butter

Toast the bread lightly, until slightly dried. Place flat in large rectangular pan.

Beat eggs and pour over toast. Let the eggs soak on one side, then turn, pressing to ensure bread soaks up all the egg mixture. Heat a non-stick frying pan and add the oil or butter to melt. Place bread in the pan (without overlapping) and cook on medium heat about 3-4 minutes per side until browned. Remove, sprinkle with cinnamon if desired. and serve with fancy sauce or syrup.

Fancy Sauce

1 cup (5 oz) (145g) fresh (or frozen and defrosted) fruit
(raspberries, strawberries, apricot, blueberries, or peaches)
2-3 tbsp all fruit jam (I use St Dalfour)

Blend fruit in blender with jam, or mash and warm slightly to serve.

Easy Peasy Power Pancakes

This is as easy as a box, but a zillion time better!

[Makes about 5-6, 4-inch pancakes]

1 large egg
1 cup (4 oz) (115g) oats
⅓ cup (1½ oz) (42g) blanched almond flour*
½ cup (4 fl oz) (120ml) coconut or dairy milk
1 tsp baking powder
2 tsp coconut sugar
1 tbsp coconut oil or butter melted

OPTIONAL TOPPINGS
dark chocolate chunks
fruit

Grind oats until fine, like flour. Then mix with almond flour, sugar and baking powder until combined. Blend eggs, milk and oil. Add flour mixture and blend until just combined.

Heat a griddle or frying pan until hot then brush on oil or butter. Pour batter into pan and cook until bubbles form on the top and when a corner is lifted the pancake is golden brown on the bottom. Flip and cook until golden brown on other side. Top with chocolate or fruit.

*To make your own almond flour, simply grind about ¾ cup of whole blanched almonds in a blender to make 1 cup almond flour. Excess almond flour can be stored in the freezer for future use.

Crepes

You'll feel as if you're in Paris...

[Makes 6]

2 large eggs
1¼ cup (10 fl oz) (260ml) unsweetened almond or dairy milk
2 tbsp extra virgin coconut oil or butter, plus a bit extra for greasing the pan
1 cup (4 oz) (115g) whole wheat pastry or sprouted wheat flour

OPTIONAL TOPPINGS
fresh fruit or all fruit jam
dark chocolate sauce for drizzling

Beat eggs until frothy. Add milk and melted butter or oil and blend until combined. Add flour and blend until smooth. (Consistency should be like heavy cream.)

Heat a non-stick small pan, or crepe pan, and brush lightly with melted butter. Pour about 1-2 oz of the crepe mixture in the pan and swirl immediately to cover the bottom lightly. Cook 1-2 minutes until little bubbles appear in the surface and when one corner is lifted, it is lightly browned. Turn and cook 1 minute on the other side. (The first crepe is often a dud. Don't worry, the rest will be fine.)

Layer crepes between parchment paper until ready to serve.

To serve, place fruit only jam and/or fruit in top right corner and then fold crepe over and over again to form a triangle. Drizzle with melted dark chocolate sauce if desired. (NOTE: These crepes are also great with savory fillings.)

Smoothie Does It

[Serves 1-2]

½ cup (2 oz) (55g) fresh or frozen mango or pineapple
1 cup (5 oz) (145g) fresh or frozen strawberries
1 banana
water to thin

Place all the fruit in a blender and blend on high, adding ¼ cup of water to thin if needed. Water can be replaced by plain yogurt or unsweetened almond milk if you fancy a creamier milkshake-like smoothie. Serve cold, slightly frozen.

savory snacks

Parmesan Crisps

[Makes roughly one dozen chips]

1 cup (4 oz) (115g) fresh Parmesan cheese, grated medium
1 tsp crushed cumin seeds or dried thyme (optional)

Mix cheese with herbs if using and spread thinly on a sheet of parchment paper. Bake at 375°F (190°C) for 8-10 minutes until lightly browned and melted. Remove from oven and let cool before breaking into chunks. Serve room temperature or store in an airtight container at room temperature. (Do not store in fridge or the chips will get soft.)

Fondue Swiss Style

1 large garlic clove, crushed
2 cups (8 oz) (225g) gruyere cheese, grated
3 cups (12 oz) (340g) Emmenthaler (quality Swiss) cheese, grated
1 tbsp cornstarch
1½ cups (12 fl oz) (375ml) dry white wine

French baguettes or sourdough bread, cubed
1 lb (16 oz) (500g) lightly sautéed whole mushrooms
1 head broccoli, lightly blanched

Rub garlic around the inside of a Dutch oven. Toss cheese with the cornstarch and then heat 8 oz of wine in the garlic-coated pan. Gradually add the cheese and stir until melted. Add more wine if needed to thin to dipping consistency. Keep warm to serve. Dip bread, mushrooms, and broccoli in the warm fondue.

Pesto Goat Cheese Dip

[Makes 1½ cups]

⅓ cup (2 oz) (55g) fresh pesto sauce (see below)
1 cup packed (8 oz) (225g) mild goat cheese
¼ cup (2 oz) (55g) plain Greek yogurt
2 tbsp extra virgin olive oil
water to thin if needed

Mix pesto, yogurt, olive oil, and goat cheese in a food processor or with electric mixer until combined. Thin to dipping consistency with water. Serve with veggies, bread, or breadsticks.

Pesto

[Makes 1 cup]

¼ cup (2 fl oz) (55g) extra virgin olive oil
juice of 1 lemon
1 cup (1 oz) (28g) fresh basil leaves
2 cups (2 oz) (55g) fresh baby spinach leaves
⅓ cup (1½ oz) (42g) pine nuts, almonds, walnuts or pistachios
½ cup (2 oz) (55g) fresh parmesan or romano, grated medium
1 large garlic clove, crushed

First pour oil and lemon juice in a blender. Then place basil, spinach, nuts, and parmesan over that and blend on medium until combined.

Cheesy Twists

1 sheet (14 oz) (400g) puff pastry
1 large egg, beaten
¼ cup (1 oz) (28g) finely grated parmesan cheese and/or
2 tbsp dried cumin, rosemary, thyme, or oregano

Brush a sheet of puff pastry with beaten egg and sprinkle with parmesan and herbs. Cut into ¼ inch wide strips. Cut in half and twist slightly, the entire length of each strip. Bake at 375°F (190°C) for 10-12 minutes until lightly browned. Serve warm or room temperature.

Homemade Pita Chips

6 whole wheat pita rounds
¼ cup (2 fl oz) (55ml) extra virgin olive oil
1 large garlic clove, crushed (optional)
1 tbsp dried thyme, oregano, cumin seed, or rosemary
1 tsp sea salt (optional)

Separate pita rounds by hand (easiest to do at room temperature or when warmed slightly). Place the single layers on a baking sheet and bake at 350°F (180°C) for 5-7 minutes or until crisp. Remove and brush with olive oil and sprinkle with garlic herb mixture or sea salt. Break into pieces and serve. Can be made ahead. Store in airtight container at room temperature.

Hummus

*This is so easy and delicious you'll never want
store-bought hummus again.*

1 cup (3 oz) (85g) chick peas or cannellini beans, cooked*
or canned, drained and rinsed
1 large garlic clove, crushed
¼ cup (2 fl oz) (55ml) freshly squeezed lemon juice
¼ cup (2 oz) (55g) tahini paste (blended sesame seeds)
2-3 tbsp extra virgin olive oil for drizzling
¼ cup (2 fl oz) (55ml) water to thin

Place all ingredients except for olive oil in a blender and blend on
high until very smooth. Transfer mixture to a dish and drizzle with
oil to serve. Serve with fresh veggies and pita chips.

*To prepare dried beans, cover with at least 4 inches of room tem-
perature water and soak at room temperature for at least 8 hours
or overnight. Drain the water and place beans in boiling water to
cover and boil for 30-35 minutes until tender. Drain to use.

Basil, Pepper & Feta Dip

[Makes about 1 ½ cups]

4 red peppers
3 tbsp extra virgin olive oil
2 medium garlic cloves, crushed
1 cup crumbled (4 oz) (115g) feta cheese
small handful fresh basil leaves
a few tbsp water to thin if needed
pita chips, whole wheat crackers, or fresh veggies to serve

Cut peppers in half, removing stems and seeds. Place peppers, cut side down, on a baking sheet and bake at 400°F (200°C) for 15-20 minutes until softened. Remove from oven, cool to room temperature, and peel off any visible skin before placing them with the garlic, oil and cheese in a processor or blender. Blend until thoroughly combined. Add basil and pulse until mixed. Thin with water to spreading consistency and serve with chips, crackers, or fresh veggies.

Sundried Tomato Dip

[Makes 1 ½ cups]

1 cup (8 oz) (250g) plain Greek yogurt
¼ cup (2 oz) (55g) pine nuts
1 cup (7 oz) (200g) sundried tomatoes, drained
¼ cup (1 oz) (28g) finely grated fresh parmesan
2 medium garlic cloves, crushed
2 handfuls fresh basil leaves, plus a bit extra to garnish

Place sundried tomatoes in a food processor and pulse until roughly chopped. Add remaining ingredients and process until combined. Place in a serving dish and garnish with extra basil and serve with zucchini chips.

Zucchini Chips

4 small zucchini
2 tbsp extra virgin olive oil

Slice zucchini, on a slight diagonal, into rounds, ¼ inch thick. Heat griddle or skillet to high. Place slices on hot pan and cook 3-4 minutes on one side, then turn and cook 2-3 minutes, or until lightly browned. These can also be baked in a 400°F (200°C) oven. Chips should be slightly softened, but still crisp. Remove zucchini from pan and toss in olive oil. Chips can be done ahead and kept at room temperature until ready to serve.

Curry Spread

You'll enjoy this yummy, versatile spread! It's great for sandwiches and salads. Or thin with a bit of water and serve with lentil chips.

1 tbsp extra virgin coconut oil
1 tbsp unsalted hot or medium curry powder
¼ cup (2 oz) (60g) fresh mango pieces, mashed
⅓ cup (1½ oz) (40g) unsalted raw sunflower seeds
3 tbsp unsalted raw cashew nuts
1 tbsp fresh finely grated ginger
1 garlic clove, crushed
juice of 1 lime

Heat oil on medium, add curry powder and cook 1 minute. Add mango and stir to combine. Place all ingredients in a blender or food processor and blend on high until combined.

You can use this curry spread to fill cabbage leaves, too. Rolled up with veggies, it's really wonderful!

Feta & Tomato Greek Nachos

2 cups (16 oz) (450g) sweet grape tomatoes, halved lengthwise
½ cup (4 oz) (115g) sundried tomatoes, drained and diced

4 whole pitas
⅓ cup (3 fl oz) (85ml) extra virgin olive oil
1 tbsp dried thyme

1 cup (4 oz) (115g) feta cheese, crumbled
3 tbsp chopped black or green olives (optional)
basil and/or thyme leaves to garnish

Brush a roasting pan with oil and roast halved tomatoes in a single layer at 325°F (170°C) for 30 minutes and remove. (These can be done a day in advance.)

Open pitas and bake at 350°F (180°C) for 5-7 minutes until crispy. Mix olive oil, garlic, and thyme and brush insides of baked pita bread. Break pitas into pieces. (These, too, can be done in advance.)

To serve, place pita pieces in a single layer on an oven proof serving platter and sprinkle with roasted tomatoes, sun dried tomatoes, feta, and olives. Bake at 350°F (180°C) for 5-7 minutes, until warm. Garnish with basil and thyme leaves.

Spicy Avocado Samosas
(or Just Plain Dip)

[Makes 1 cup dip]

2 large avocados, pitted and peeled
juice of 1 lime
3 tbsp sundried tomatoes, chopped
3 tbsp red onion, chopped finely
1 tbsp extra virgin coconut oil
1 tbsp unsalted curry powder

FOR SAMOSAS
[Makes 12-15]

6 sheets filo pastry
2 tbsp extra virgin coconut oil, melted

Coarsely mash avocados with lime juice. Mix in tomatoes, and onion. Heat a tbsp of oil with curry powder about 2-3 minutes until fragrant, then add to the avocado mixture. Dip can be served with puppodums, lentil chips, or used as a filling in samosas or sushi rolls.

TO MAKE SAMOSAS: Divide filo into 3 stacks of two sheets each. Brush coconut oil between layers, where possible. Cut each stack into 4-5 short strips. Place a tbsp of avocado mixture at the top right hand corner of each strip and fold diagonally, enclosing the filling, to form a triangle. Continue folding, maintaining a triangular shape until you reach the end of the strip. Brush with oil and place seamside down on parchment paper. (These can be made ahead and frozen. Defrost before baking.)

Bake at 375°F (190°C) for 12-15 minutes until lightly browned and crisped. Serve warm or room temperature.

Pumpkin Dip

This festive autumn dip is sure to impress and is a clever trick and treat!

[Makes 1 pumpkin bowl]

1 small pie pumpkin
1 cup packed (8 oz) (225g) garlic & herb goat cheese
¾ cup (6 fl oz) (170ml) boiling water
4 tbsp fresh herbs like thyme, rosemary, or sage
½ cup (2 oz) (55g) fresh parmesan cheese, grated finely

Wash pumpkin. Cut off the top and reserve. Clean out the seeds and gunk inside pumpkin. (Seeds can be dried and roasted for munching later.)

Mix cheese and water first, then add the herbs and parmesan. Pour inside the pumpkin. Put the top on the pumpkin and place the filled pumpkin on a baking sheet. Bake at 375°F (190°C) for 35-45 minutes until the pumpkin is lightly browned and softened. Remove and let sit with top off for 15 minutes to cool and thicken. Serve with crackers or veggies. Be sure to spoon out some of the pumpkin flesh to eat with the dip!

Fresh Italian Bean Dip

[Makes 2½ cups]

2 cups (6 oz) (170g) cannellini beans, cooked* or canned
2 medium tomatoes, chopped
3 tbsp fresh thyme, oregano, rosemary, and/or basil, chopped
1 red chili deseeded, deveined and chopped
(for less heat, remove white vein on underside)
2 medium garlic cloves, crushed
3 tbsp fresh lemon juice
5 tbsp extra virgin olive oil
sea salt to taste

Mix all ingredients together and serve with pita chips.

*To prepare dried beans, cover with at least 4 inches of room temperature water and soak at room temperature for at least 8 hours or overnight. Drain the water and place beans in boiling water and boil for 30-35 minutes until tender. Drain to use.

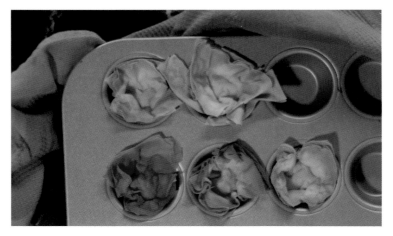

Braised Cabbage in Filo Baskets

[Makes 24]

2 tbsp extra virgin coconut oil or olive oil
1 tbsp dried herbs
8 large sheets filo pastry

½ medium sweet onion, sliced finely
½ head red cabbage, cut very finely
½ cup (4 fl oz) (125ml) balsamic vinegar
1 tbsp finely chopped rosemary or sage leaves
2 large garlic cloves, crushed
1 heaping tbsp fresh ginger root, grated finely
¾ cup (4 oz) (115g) whole pecans, plain or spicy
½ cup (4 oz) (115g) goat cheese, crumbled
rosemary to garnish

Heat a Dutch oven and add onion. Cover and sauté on low heat until softened. Add cabbage, balsamic vinegar, rosemary or sage, garlic and ginger. Heat to boiling, then cover and place in the oven at 350°F (180°C) for 1 hour. (Check the mixture half way through to see if it is too dry and if it is add a little water to moisten.) Remove when mixture is reduced and softened. (This can be prepared a day in advance.)

TO MAKE TARTS: Separate filo pastry into 2 stacks of 4 layers each; brush a little coconut oil and dried herbs between each layer. Cut each stack into squares, slightly larger than your muffin cups. Press each into ungreased cups. Bake at 375°F (190°C) for about 5 minutes until lightly browned. (These can be done days in advance and stored at room temperature.)

To serve warm cabbage mixture and fill baskets. Top with crumbled cheese, nuts and a sprig of rosemary.

Pesto Palmiers

[Serves 8-10]

1 sheet (14 oz) (400g) puff pastry
6 heaping tbsp fresh pesto
4 tbsp chopped, thawed artichoke hearts
¼ cup (1 oz) (28g) freshly grated parmesan

Line a baking sheet with parchment paper. Roll out pastry so that it's ⅛ inch thick; lay sheet on parchment and spread the pesto, artichokes, and parmesan over the pastry. Roll from the long side to halfway of the width and then roll the opposite side in to meet the first side. Freeze at least 20 minutes and then cut across into ½ inch slices. Bake, cut side up, at 375°F (190°C) for 15-18 minutes until lightly browned. Serve warm. (Log can be kept frozen and cut and cooked at a later time.)

FRESH PESTO
¼ cup (2 fl oz) (55g) extra virgin olive oil
juice of 1 lemon
1 cup (1 oz) (28g) fresh basil leaves
2 cups (2 oz) (55g) fresh baby spinach leaves
⅓ cup (1½ oz) (42g) pine nuts, almonds, walnuts or pistachios
½ cup (2 oz) (55g) fresh parmesan or romano, medium grated
1 large garlic clove, crushed

First pour oil and lemon juice in a blender. Then place basil, spinach, nuts, and parmesan over that and blend on medium until combined.

Garlic Herb Cheese Rounds with Mountain Cherry Rosemary Chutney

[Makes 8-10 rounds]

6 slices whole wheat or sprouted bread
1 log (11 oz) (310g) garlic and herb goat cheese
small dish of flour
2 large eggs, beaten
1 tbsp dried thyme
2-3 tbsp extra virgin coconut oil for sautéeing

Toast bread and grind in blender to make bread crumbs. Set aside.

Cut cheese into 1 inch thick rounds. Roll first in flour, then dip in egg mixture, then roll in bread crumbs. Freeze rounds until firm, at least 30 minutes. Heat oil in a large frying pan until hot. Place frozen cheese patties at least 1 inch apart and cook about 2-3 minutes until browned on 1 side. Turn over carefully to brown on the other side. Remove and drain on paper towels.

CHUTNEY
½ cup (2 oz) (55g) dried unsweetened cherries
¼ cup (2 fl oz) (55ml) balsamic vinegar
1 tbsp fresh rosemary, chopped finely
1 large garlic clove, crushed
2 tbsp all fruit black cherry preserves

Place cherries, vinegar, rosemary, garlic, and jam in a saucepan and bring to a boil. Simmer about 5 minutes until thickened. Cool and reserve. To serve, top each cheese round with a little chutney.

Mozzarella Balls

[Makes approx 20-25]

6 slices whole wheat or sprouted bread, toasted
2 large eggs, beaten
1 cup (4 oz) (115g) whole wheat, sprouted wheat, or spelt flour
1 heaping tbsp dried oregano
20-25 mozzarella balls (fresh buffalo if possible) drained
2-3 tbsp extra virgin coconut oil for sautéeing

SAUCE FOR DIPPING
1 jar (24 oz) (680g) vine ripened tomatoes
7 oz (200g) tomato paste
2 large garlic cloves, crushed

Place bread in a blender, grind until fine breadcrumbs. Set out 3 bowls and fill one with eggs, another with flour, and another with the breadcrumbs and dried oregano. Roll each mozzarella ball first in flour, then egg, and lastly in breadcrumbs. Freeze balls at least 20 minutes, or up to 2 months.

Heat oil in frying pan until hot then place mozzarella balls in the pan with about 1 inch between each ball. This may require several batches; add more oil as necessary between batches. Cook quickly until completely browned and drain on paper towels.

For sauce, place all ingredients in a blender and blend until smooth. Heat in a saucepan on medium heat for 5 minutes to reduce slightly. Sauce can be made days in advance and rewarmed to serve with the mozzarella balls. (Sauce can be used for pasta or turkey meatballs, too.)

Mexican Roll Ups

[Serves 8-10]

½ cup (4 oz) (115g) cream cheese
1 cup (4 oz) (115g) sharp cheddar cheese, grated
1 cup (8 oz) (250g) plain Greek yogurt
3 spring onions, sliced
½ tsp red chili flakes (optional)
5 whole wheat, spelt, or sprouted flour tortillas
2 avocados, pitted, peeled and diced
juice of 1 lime
1 large handful fresh baby spinach leaves
salsa for dipping

Mix the cheeses, yogurt, onions, and chili flakes in a bowl. Spread this mixture about ¼ of an inch thick over each tortilla. Toss avocados in lime juice and place over cheese mixture. Cover with spinach leaves and roll each tortilla as tightly as possible. Wrap each tightly in parchment paper and chill 8-12 hours or overnight before serving. To serve unwrap and slice into 1 inch slices across the roll and serve cut side up with salsa for dipping.

Cranberry Brie Slice

[Makes 12-15 slices]

1 sweet onion, sliced thinly
1 sheet (14 oz) (400g) puff pastry
½ cup (4 oz) (115g) cranberry sauce
½ tbsp fresh finely chopped rosemary leaves
2 pie-shaped wedges (8 oz) (225g) triple cream brie, sliced with rind

Place onion in covered pan and cook on low until softened, about 7-10 minutes. Remove and reserve. Place pastry sheet on parchment paper lined baking sheet and roll to ⅛ inch thick. Mix cranberry sauce with the rosemary and spread two thirds of it over the pastry. Top this with the onions and then the cheese slices. (This can be done ahead and chilled until ready to bake.)

To serve, remove from fridge 30 minutes before baking and bake at 350°F (180°C) near the bottom of the oven for 25-30 minutes until puffed and golden brown. Remove and let rest 5 minutes before drizzling with the rest of the cranberry sauce. Cut into squares to serve warm.

CRANBERRY SAUCE
½ cup (2 oz) (55g) fresh or frozen cranberries
¼ cup (2 fl oz) (55g) water or fruity red wine or port
2 tbsp all fruit raspberry jam

Combine all ingredients in blender. Transfer to sauce pan and bring to boil. Then lower heat and cook for 10 minutes until cranberries are softened and sauce has thickened.

Spicy Poached Pear Tartlets

An unusual twist on poached pears!

[Makes 12-15]

2 cinnamon sticks
2 tbsp fresh ginger, grated finely
½ bottle (1½ cups) (375ml) fruity dry red wine
3 tbsp all fruit raspberry jam
1-2 red or green hot chilis, deseeded and sliced horizontally
3 tbsp of juice from an orange
juice of 1 lime
3 pears, peeled and cut in half horizontally
1 sheet (14 oz) (400g) puff pastry
½ cup (2 oz) (55g) humbodlt fog, goat, or blue cheese crumbles

Mix cinnamon, ginger, wine, jam, orange, lime and chili in a large saucepan and bring to a boil. Add pears and simmer uncovered for about 45 minutes until sauce is reduced and pears are tender. Cool pears in liquid, then remove. Reserve sauce. Slice pears. Boil sauce until thickened and set aside. Roll pastry to ⅛ inch thick and cut into 2-3-inch rounds. Place on parchment lined baking sheet and bake at 375°F (190°C) for about 12-15 minutes until lightly golden. Fan pear slices on rounds, drizzle with sauce, and garnish with cheese. Serve warm or make ahead and rewarm to serve.

salads

soups

Dad's Caesar Salad

[Serves 4]

2 tbsp extra virgin olive oil
1 large clove garlic, crushed
6 tomatoes, chopped
1 bunch green onions, chopped
1 large or 2 small heads romaine lettuce, chopped

DRESSING
½ cup (4 fl oz) (115ml) extra virgin olive oil
juice from 2 lemons
1 large tbsp fresh mint
1 tsp fresh or ½ tsp dried oregano
2 large garlic cloves, crushed
2 tbsp plain Greek yogurt
¾ cup (3 oz) (85g) fresh parmesan, grated finely

CROUTONS
3 slices sprouted or whole wheat bread, such as Ezekiel
¼ cup (2 fl oz) (55ml) extra virgin olive
1 large garlic clove, crushed
freshly ground black pepper to taste

FOR SALAD: Rub salad bowl with 1 crushed clove of garlic and a little olive oil. Then add, in this order: tomatoes, onions, and lettuce.

FOR DRESSING: Put oil, lemon juice, garlic, yogurt and ¼ cup (1 oz) (28g) grated parmesan in a blender and blend on high until creamy. Mix in oregano and mint.

FOR CROUTONS: Toast bread in the oven at 350°F (180°C) for 5-7 minutes until crisp and lightly browned. Mix 1 clove garlic with ¼ cup oil and spread each side of bread lightly with the olive oil garlic mixture. Cut or break into small pieces and set aside.

(Both the croutons and the dressing can be done a few days in advance. Store dressing in an airtight container and refrigerate. Store croutons an airtight container, but do not refrigerate or they will get soggy!)

TO SERVE: Toss salad with only enough dressing to coat the leaves. (Too much dressing ruins a Caesar salad.) A great way to do this is Julia Child's way: Use your hands! Add croutons, reserved parmesan and black pepper to taste.

Kale Caesar

[Serves 4]

4 cups (4 oz) (115g) kale leaves (fresh as possible to
avoid bitter taste)
1 large garlic clove, crushed
1 tbsp extra virgin olive oil
pinch red pepper flakes
2 tsp cumin seeds

DRESSING
¼ cup (2 fl oz) (55ml) freshly squeezed lemon juice
1 large garlic clove, crushed
¼ cup (1 oz) (28g) fresh parmesan, grated finely
½ cup (4 fl oz) (115ml) extra virgin olive oil

CRISPY ONIONS (optional)
2 shallots, skinned and very sliced thinly
4 tbsp extra virgin coconut oil

CUMIN PARMESAN CRISPS (optional)
1 tsp cumin seeds
½ cup (2 oz) (55g) fresh parmesan, grated medium

To prepare kale leaves, remove tough center stems. Place in food processor or blender to chop into very small pieces. Rub 1 clove of garlic crushed with a tbsp of olive oil in a salad bowl. Add prepared kale.

In a dry frying pan, warm cumin seeds and red pepper, then bash them a bit with a rolling pin or mortar and pestle and set aside.

FOR DRESSING: Place lemon juice, garlic, ¼ cup (1 oz) of parmesan, and oil in a blender and blend until combined and thickened.

FOR CRISPY ONIONS: Heat coconut oil in a medium saucepan until hot then add shallots and cook on high until crispy. To ensure they are crispy, press between paper towels to remove grease.

CUMIN PARMESAN CRISPS: Sprinkle grated parmesan and cumin seeds over non stick baking parchment and bake at 375°F (190°C) for 5-7 minutes until melted and lightly browned. Remove and let cool then break into pieces to serve.

TO SERVE: Add just enough dressing to lightly coat kale. Do this using your hands which is the best way to massage the dressing into the leaves. Mix cumin and pepper mixture into greens. Top with crispy onions, and cumin parmesan crisps.

Tabbouli

Try this stuffed into zucchini or grape leaves and baked.

[Makes 6-8 servings]

¼ cup (1¼ oz) (38g) quinoa
½ cup (4 fl oz) (115ml) boiling water
3 cups (2 large bunches) flat leaf parsley, tough stems removed
3 tbsp chopped fresh mint leaves
2 large tomatoes, diced finely
½ yellow or sweet onion, diced finely
freshly squeezed juice from 2 lemons
⅓ cup (3 fl oz) (85ml) extra virgin olive oil
sea salt to taste
romaine leaves for serving

Pour boiling water over the quinoa and heat on low covered for about 7-10 minutes just until slightly softened. Drain any excess water and set aside. Wash and dry parsley thoroughly and remove any thick stems. (A salad spinner and tea towel are ideal for this.) Chop parsley by hand or use a processor, pulsing parsley until finely chopped, but not mushy. Place parsley, mint, tomato, and onion in a bowl and add quinoa. Mix in lemon juice, olive oil, and sea salt to taste. Chill. Serve with romaine leaves for scooping.

Satay Salad

This recipe was declared delicious by men who hate salad. Great way to create a fab meal and use leftover veggies, too!

[Serves 4-6]

FOR SALAD
½ head green cabbage, finely shredded
½ red onion, diced finely
2 stalks broccoli, chopped finely
3 tbsp cilantro leaves, chopped finely
3 tbsp thai basil, chopped finely or 1½ tbsp each basil and mint
2 avocados, pitted, peeled and cut into pieces
½ fresh mango, chopped finely
¾ cup (4 oz) (115g) almond, cashew, or macadamia pieces for garnish

SAUCE
2 tbsp unseasoned rice vinegar
juice of ½ lime
2 tbsp extra virgin coconut oil
3 tbsp unsalted peanut butter or almond butter
3 tbsp fresh mango, mashed
1 tbsp fresh ginger, peeled and finely grated
1 clove garlic, minced
about ¼ cup (2 fl oz) (55ml) water to thin

Mix cabbage, onion, broccoli, cilantro and basil in a bowl. Place all the sauce ingredients except for water in a blender and blend until smooth. Add enough water to thin to pouring consistency. Toss with the cabbage mixture and fold in avocado and mango. Garnish with nuts if desired.

Upside Down Salad

[Serves 4]

½ cup (3 oz) (85g) raw walnut pieces
2 Barlett or Anjou pears
juice of 1 lime
1-1½ cups (4-6 oz) (140-175g) mild goat cheese, crumbled
¼ cup (1 oz) (28g) dried cranberries
3 cups (3 oz) (85g) mixed leaf lettuce

DRESSING
2 tbsp walnut oil
¼ cup (2 fl oz) (55ml) extra virgin olive oil
3 tbsp sherry vinegar
½ tsp Dijon mustard

Soak walnuts in room temperature water for 1-2 hours to remove bitter taste. Drain, dry and set aside.

Cut pears in ¼ inch slices and toss with lime juice to keep them from turning brown.

Blend all the dressing ingredients in a blender and set aside.

Scatter pear slices over a large serving plate and drizzle with a little dressing. Top with half the walnuts, cranberries and cheeses. Toss the leaves with enough of the dressing to coat lightly and pile on top of the pear mixture. Sprinkle remaining walnuts, cranberries and cheese on top.

Roasted Sweet Potato & Green Bean Salad with Manchego & Pine Nuts

[Serves 4-6]

2 medium-sized (1¼ lb) (575g) sweet potatoes
2 tbsp extra virgin coconut oil
½ cup (3 oz) (85g) pine nuts, lightly toasted
1-1½ cups (4-6 oz) (110-175g) aged manchego cheese
2 cups (8 oz) (225g) French green beans, topped and tailed

DRESSING
6 tbsp extra virgin olive oil
3 tbsp balsamic vinegar
1 tbsp fresh lemon juice
1 large garlic clove, crushed

Pierce potatoes with a fork in several places and bake at 375°F (190°C) for about 30 minutes just until tender. Remove from the oven and remove skins immediately so that juices don't accumulate. Cool and cut into 1 inch pieces. Toss with warm coconut oil and place in roasting pan and bake at 400°F (200°C) for about 15-20 minutes until lightly browned. Remove and set aside. (Potatoes can be prepared a day before.)

FOR DRESSING: Blend oil, vinegar, lemon juice and garlic in a blender until creamy and set aside. (Can be prepared a day before.)

TO SERVE: Warm potatoes and beans at 375° (190°C) about 5-10 minutes. Toss with enough dressing just to coat. Mound beans and potatoes on a serving plate. Shave manchego cheese using a vegetable peeler over the vegetables. Garnish with pine nuts. Serve warm or at room temperature.

Spinach, Avocado, Feta & Pomegranate Salad

[Serves 4-6]

3 tbsp extra virgin coconut oil
4 shallots sliced thinly
3 cups (5 oz) (145g) fresh baby spinach leaves
2 large avocados, pitted and peeled
juice of 1 lime
seeds from ½ pomegranate

DRESSING
¼ cup (2 fl oz) (55ml) sherry vinegar
½ cup (4 fl oz) (115ml) extra virgin olive oil
1 large garlic clove, crushed
½ cup (2 oz) (55g) feta cheese, crumbled

Heat oil until very hot in a frying pan and stirfry shallots until lightly browned. Remove and drain on paper towels. (These can be made ahead and stored at room temperature.)

FOR DRESSING: Combine vinegar, oil, garlic, and feta in a blender until creamy.

TO SERVE: Slice avocados. (Drench with lime juice to keep them from turning brown.) Lightly coat spinach with dressing. Top with avocado, pomegranate and prepared shallots. Serve at room temperature.

Spinach Raspberry Salad

[Serves 4-6]

1 cup (4 oz) (115g) thin French green beans, topped and tailed
3 cups (3 oz) (85g) fresh baby spinach
1 cup (5 oz) (145g) fresh raspberries
½ cup (2 oz) (55g) slivered almonds, lightly warmed
1½ cup (6 oz) (170g) goat cheese, crumbled

DRESSING
½ cup (4 fl oz) (115ml) extra virgin olive oil
¼ cup (2 fl oz) (55ml) balsamic vinegar
6 fresh raspberries
½ tsp Dijon mustard
1 tsp coconut sugar

Blend dressing ingredients in a blender until creamy and set aside.

Steam beans for about 2 minutes and refresh under cold water to preserve crispness and color. Toss spinach leaves, half the raspberries, and beans with just enough dressing to coat and place on a serving platter. Garnish with nuts, cheese, and remaining raspberries. Serve room temperature.

SPINACH

Spinach, a native plant of Persia (modern day Iran) is best eaten fresh. Spinach has a high nutritional value and is extremely rich in vitamins, minerals, especially folic acid, soluable fiber, and antioxidants that protect against oxygen-derived free radicals. Eating healthy greens helps improve learning and motor skills and reduces brain aging.

However, spinach also contains a high concentration of oxalic acid which can be responsible for the formation of kidney stones. A little trick to reduce the negative impact of oxylic acid is to combine spinach with dairy products such as goat or feta cheese.

I love the convenience of bagged spinach, and I always buy organic spinach to avoid exposure to pesticides. When possible try the lush bunches at your local farmers' market or plant some yourself. Spinach grows quickly and can be harvested and eaten in only 37 to 45 days!

To learn more about avoiding toxins when buying produce, check out: www.ewg.org/foodnews/

Arugula Salad with Strawberries & Pistachios

[Serves 4-6]

DRESSING
½ cup (4 fl oz) (125ml) white wine vinegar
¼ cup (2 fl oz) (60ml) fresh orange juice
½ cup (4 fl oz) (125ml) extra virgin olive oil

SALAD
1 avocado, pitted, peeled and sliced thinly
juice of 1 lime3 cups (3oz) (85g) baby arugula
⅓ sweet onion, sliced thinly
1 cup (5 oz) (145g) sliced fresh strawberries
½ cup (3 oz) (85g) raw shelled pistachios

FOR THE DRESSING: Reduce vinegar and orange juice by placing it in a small saucepan, no more than 1 inch deep. Boil on medium high for 4-5 minutes until thickened and reduced by about half. Mix 4-5 tbsp of reduced vinegar with oil to taste. Reserve remaining vinegar for brushing on grilled meats or veggies.

FOR THE SALAD: Slice avocado and drench with lime juice to keep from turning brown. Toss arugula and onions with dressing to lightly coat. Mound dressed greens on a serving plate and top with avocado, strawberries, and pistachios. Drizzle with a little dressing. Serve at room temperature for best flavor.

Warm Red Cabbage Salad

[Serves 4]

1 cup (1 small) red onion, sliced very thinly
4 cups (1 small) red cabbage, sliced very thinly
1 apple with skin, grated medium
3 dried figs, grated medium
¼ cup (1 oz) (28g) raisins
½ cup (4 fl oz) (125ml) balsamic vinegar
½ cup (4 fl oz) (125ml) water
3 medium garlic cloves, crushed
1 heaping tbsp fresh ginger, grated finely

Heat Dutch oven and sauté onions covered on low until softened. Add rest of the ingredients and bring to a boil. Cover and place in the oven at 350°F (180°C) for 45-60 minutes, stirring halfway through. Can be served as is or with spinach or arugula tossed through and dotted with goat cheese. Can be made ahead and re-warmed.

Mojo Chicken Salad

[Serves 4]

MARINADE
1 tbsp cumin seeds
6 large garlic cloves
¼ cup (2 fl oz) (55ml) melted extra virgin coconut oil
¼ cup (2 fl oz) (55ml) orange juice, freshly squeezed
¼ cup (2 fl oz) (55ml) lime juice, freshly squeezed

DRESSING
½ cup (4 fl oz) (125ml) extra virgin olive oil
¼ (2 fl oz) (60ml) cup fresh orange juice
½ tbsp honey
½ tbsp soy sauce
1 tbsp freshly minced ginger
juice of 1 lime
1 medium garlic clove, crushed

SALAD
2 single chicken breasts boned, skinned, and sliced
1 cup (5 oz) (145g) mango pieces
2 medium avocados, pitted, peeled and sliced
3 cups (3 oz) (85g) mixed salad leaves
3 green onions, cut into thin strips
4 tbsp freshly chopped cilantro to garnish
juice of 1 lime, plus 1 lime, cut into 8 wedges
½ cup (2 oz) (55g) cashew pieces

FOR MARINADE: Heat cumin seeds just until warm and then mix in the rest of the marinade ingredients. Submerge the chicken in the marinade and leave it at least an hour, or up to 1 day, in fridge.

FOR DRESSING: Combine ingredients in a blender and set aside.

FOR SALAD: Remove chicken from the marinade and bake in a roasting pan for 15-20 minutes at 400°F (200°C) until juices run clear when pierced. Let rest for about 5 minutes and then cut each breast into thin slices. Toss lettuce with enough dressing to lightly coat and arrange the leaves on a platter or on individual plates. Toss the avocado and mango in some lime juice and arrange down each side of the lettuce. Arrange the chicken in the middle, drizzle with dressing, and top with green onions, cashews, and cilantro to garnish. Serve with extra lime pieces.

Chicken Salad Fit for a Queen

A favorite in England, this was originally made for the coronation of Queen Elizabeth. I have reconfigured it, making it a bit more healthy without cheating on taste so dig in and enjoy!

[Serves 4]

2 chicken breasts, skinned and deboned
1 cup (8 fl oz) (250ml) low sodium chicken broth
1 tbsp hot curry powder
1 tbsp extra virgin coconut oil
⅓ sweet onion, diced finely
1 tbsp unsalted tomato paste
juice from 1 lemon
4 tbsp all fruit apricot jam
4 tbsp plain Greek yogurt
1 red pepper, chopped finely
1 medium bunch lightly steamed broccoli, cut in small pieces
4 green onions, chopped finely
4 tbsp cilantro, chopped finely
½ cup (2 oz) (55g) sliced toasted almonds

Boil chicken breast in broth for 20 minutes and then cool in the broth for 10 minutes. Reserve broth and dice cooled chicken.

Heat oil in a frying pan and sauté onion on low until softened, about 5 minutes. Add curry powder and cook one minute. Stir in ½ cup reserved broth, tomato paste, lemon juice, and jam. Bring to a boil and cook for 10 minutes until thickened. Cool mixture to room temperature.

When cooled, add yogurt then broccoli, pepper, green onions, chicken, and most of the cilantro. Garnish with almonds and remaining cilantro. Serve on a bed of salad greens or a puppodum.

(Puppodums are crispy lentil tortillas. Look for Sharwoods brand in your international aisle. One minute in the microwave and they're ready!) Or roll in a rice wrapper, or whole wheat tortilla.

Grilled Asparagus, Chicken & Avocado Salad with Warm Lemon Hollandaise

[Serves 4]

1 tbsp extra virgin coconut oil
2 chicken breasts skinless
2 cups (16 oz) (450g) sweet cherry tomatoes
1 bunch of asparagus with woody ends broken off
2 avocados, pitted, peeled and sliced thinly
4-6 cups (5 oz) (140 g) mixed salad leaves
1 tbsp lemon juice
2 tbsp extra virgin olive oil
½ medium red onion, sliced thinly

DRESSING
2 large egg yolks
3 tbsp water
5 tbsp extra virgin coconut oil or butter
2 tbsp lemon juice
1 tsp Dijon mustard
sea salt and black pepper

Rub roasting pan with 1 tbsp coconut oil and place chicken breasts in pan with the tomatoes scattered around them. Bake at 375°F (190°C) for about 20-25 minutes, depending on thickness of the breasts, until the juices just run clear. (Do not overcook or they will be tough and dry.) Put asparagus in with the chicken for the last 3 minutes to lightly cook. Remove from the oven and let rest for 5 minutes before thinly slicing the chicken breasts across. Set aside.

FOR THE HOLLANDAISE: place the egg yolks, water, mustard, and lemon juice in a blender and blend until combined. In a saucepan, heat the coconut oil or butter until very hot. With blender running, slowly pour the oil into the egg mixture until thoroughly combined and set aside. Warm slightly to thicken but do not overheat or the sauce will separate.

TO SERVE: Mix the olive oil and lemon juice and toss with the lettuce and onion. Place the leaves on a platter and arrange avocados, tomatoes, asparagus and chicken over the leaves. Drizzle the hollandaise dressing over the salad. Top with fresh ground black pepper.

NOTE: For a different sauce, add fresh chopped tarragon, basil or thyme to the hollandaise. This is wonderful over eggs, fish, and vegetables.

Feta, Sweet Grape Tomato & Shrimp Salad with Lemon Pesto Vinaigrette

[Serves 4-6]

1½ tbsp extra virgin coconut oil
1 lb (450g) (10-16 count) raw large shrimp, peeled and deveined
16 oz (225g) sweet grape tomatoes, halved
½ cup (3 oz) (85g) pine nuts, lightly warmed
6 cups (5 oz) (140g) mixed lettuce leaves
⅔ cup (3 oz) (85g) crumbled feta cheese or shaved parmesan cheese
½ red onion, sliced very thinly
2 avocados, pitted, peeled, sliced and tossed in juice of 1 lime

DRESSING
⅓ cup (3 fl oz) (85ml) fresh lemon juice
⅔ cup (6 fl oz) (170ml) extra virgin olive oil
1 large garlic clove, crushed
3 tbsp fresh pesto*

Heat 1 tbsp of oil in a frying pan until hot and then add shrimp and cook until just pink, about 3-4 minutes. Remove from pan and set aside. Rub a roasting pan with coconut oil and lay halved cherry tomatoes, cut side up, and bake at 325°F (170°C) for 30-35 minutes until slightly shriveled. (These can be done a day in advance.) Warm pine nuts in a dry frying pan until lightly warmed and remove. In a blender, mix all the dressing ingredients until combined and set aside. To assemble salad, toss greens, half the cheese and onions lightly in enough dressing to coat and mound on a platter. Top with the tomatoes, shrimp, pine nuts, avocado and the rest of the cheese. Drizzle dressing over.

See page 17.

Hard to Beat Beet Salad

[Serves 4-6]

3-4 beets with tops intact
3 tbsp extra virgin coconut oil
2 medium sweet onions, skinned and cut into wedges
2 cups (2 oz) (55g) fresh baby spinach
½ cup (3 oz) (85g) unsalted pistachios, crushed lightly

DRESSING
4 tbsp sherry vinegar
½ cup (4 fl oz) (125ml) extra virgin olive oil
1 large garlic clove, crushed
1 tbsp fresh or 1 tsp dried thyme leaves
1 cup (4 oz) (115g) feta or goat cheese, crumbled

Cut leaves from the root part of beets and reserve for greens. Peel the beets and then cut into wedges. Reserve good leaves and place in a bowl of cold water; chill until needed. Heat oil, split between two roasting pans and toss onion wedges in one and beet wedges in the other. This will ensure the color of the beets does not bleed on the onions. Roast both at 375°F (190°C) for about 30 minutes. Remove the onions and roast beets for another 10 minutes, or until tender. Remove and set aside. Blend vinegar, olive oil, and garlic until combined and then add thyme. Remove beet leaves, pat dry. Toss beet leaves and spinach with a bit of dressing and then toss a little dressing with the onions and beets. Place on a platter. and garnish with the cheese and pistachios.

Quickie Tomato Soup

[Serves 4]

2 cups (16 oz) (450g) crushed tomatoes
2 large garlic cloves, crushed
¾ cup (7 oz) (200g) tomato paste
½ cup fresh basil leaves (optional)
1½ cups (12 fl oz) (375ml) low sodium vegetable stock
fresh basil and croutons to garnish

Combine crushed tomatoes, garlic and tomato paste in a blender with enough stock to ensure it blends completely. Place the mixture in a saucepan and heat for 10-15 minutes on high, adding more stock to make a soup consistency. Serve with chopped basil and croutons as garnish.

Tomato Pesto Soup

[Serves 4]

1 tsp extra virgin coconut oil
2 large garlic cloves, crushed
6 large, or 12 medium, tomatoes, sliced
water to thin
sea salt to taste

Pesto
¼ cup (2 fl oz) (60ml) extra virgin olive oil
juice of 1 lemon
1 large handful fresh basil leaves
2 large handfuls fresh baby spinach leaves or kale
⅓ cup (1½) (42g) pine nuts, almonds, walnuts or pistachios
½ cup (2 oz) (55g) medium grated parmesan
1 large garlic clove, crushed

Place sliced tomatoes single layer in a large oil greased roasting pan and roast at 325°F (170°C) oven for 1 hour until shriveled. When cooled, place tomatoes and garlic in a blender and purée until smooth, adding some water as you go to loosen the mixture. Transfer to a saucepan and simmer for 15 minutes, thinning to desired consistency with water. Add sea salt to taste.

FOR THE PESTO: place the oil, and lemon in the bottom of a blender and place the basil, spinach, nuts, and parmesan over them and blend on medium just until combined. Serve soup warm or hot with the pesto drizzled over.

Seafood Gazpacho

Hailed as the best gazpacho ever by a certain CIA executive!

[Serves 4-6]

28 oz can Muir organic fire-roasted tomatoes
2 tsp cumin powder
juice of 1 lime
2 tbsp sherry vinegar
½ red pepper
2 garlic cloves, crushed
⅓ red onion
2 tbsp extra virgin olive oil
2 small cucumbers, peeled

CILANTRO OIL

1 large handful cilantro leaves
2 tbsp extra virgin olive oil
juice of ½ lime
1 small garlic clove, crushed

GARNISH

use any of these: cooked shrimp, crab,
avocado, pitted, peeled, chopped and tossed in lime juice,
red onion, roasted sweet grape tomatoes, or cilantro

Place all ingredients for the gazpacho except the cucumber in the blender and blend until combined. Then add the cucumber and blend just till combined, but still slightly chunky. Chill overnight or for at least 4 hours. Blend cilantro oil ingredients in the blender and drizzle over the soup. Serve with your choice of garnishes.

Roasted Butternut Squash Soup

This soup is an all time favorite of my dear friend Patty who eats it morning, noon, and night during the autumn! (Add less stock and you can use this as an easy yummy sauce to use with chicken or pork.)

[Serves 4-6]

1 butternut squash
1½ cups (12 fl oz) (37ml) low sodium chicken, vegetable broth
or water
1 tbsp extra virgin coconut oil
4-5 fresh sage leaves
¼ cup (2 fl oz) (60ml) balsamic vinegar
½ tsp sea salt or cumin for seeds
crumbled goat cheese or humbodlt fog to garnish

Remove top and bottom of squash and peel outside skin with a vegetable peeler. Cut in half and remove seeds. (Save for roasting.) Scrape clean and cut into large wedges. Brush a roasting pan with 2 tbsp of oil. Place squash in pan and bake at 375°F (190°C) for 40-50 minutes until lightly browned and fork tender. Place baked squash in a blender with enough stock or water to blend to a smooth purée. Add the sage in the blender at the end just to pulse in lightly, but not purée. Pour into a saucepan and add enough stock or water to achieve soup consistency and heat to serve.

TO TOAST SEEDS: bake at 375°F (190°C) for 5 minutes until golden brown. Add sea salt or cumin and a little oil for flavor at the end if desired.

FOR THE VINEGAR: heat vinegar ½ inch deep in a saucepan on high heat until reduced and syrupy. This should take less than 5 minutes and will thicken more when cooled. It can also be done in the microwave on high for 1 minute. Then stir and let set for another minute to thicken. Drizzle over the soup and sprinkle with roasted squash seeds and cheese to garnish.

Wild Mushroom Soup

[Serves 4-6]

1 oz dried mushrooms, rinsed in water to remove grit
⅔ cup (5 fl oz) (155ml) Madeira wine
2 medium shallots, chopped finely
1½ lbs. (675g) Cremini or baby bella mushrooms, sliced
2 cups (16 fl oz) (450ml) low sodium vegetable stock or water
1 tbsp chopped fresh rosemary
2 garlic cloves, crushed

GARNISH
1 tbsp Madeira wine
4 tbsp plain Greek yogurt
4-6 small sprigs of fresh rosemary to garnish (optional)

Rinse mushrooms, then pour Madeira wine over them and soak for 1 hour. In a sauce pan, soften the shallots on medium heat in a covered pan (to hold in moisture) for about 4-5 minutes. Then add fresh mushrooms, garlic, rosemary and cook for 5 minutes until softened. Remove mushrooms from the Madeira and add to the soup pan. Pour in the Madeira, but not any sediment. Add enough stock (about 5-8 oz) to cover the mixture and cover. Cook 20-30 minutes until very soft. Pour the mixture into a blender and blend until smooth, thinning with vegetable stock or water to desired soup consistency.

TO SERVE: Mix yogurt with 1 tsp of Madeira and drizzle over the top of the soup. Garnish with rosemary leaves.

Strawberry Soup

[Serves 4-6]

3 cups (1 lb) (450 g) fresh or frozen strawberries
1 tbsp all fruit strawberry jam
1 tsp vanilla paste
1½ cups (12 fl oz) (375 ml) water

YOGURT SWIRL
⅓ cup (3 oz) (85g) vanilla or plain Greek yogurt
½ tsp vanilla paste

Remove stems from berries and liquify in blender or food processor with water and vanilla.*

YOGURT SWIRL
Blend yogurt and vanilla until smooth.

Spoon soup into bows and swirl a little yogurt on top. Garnish with mint leaves.

*ADULT VERSION: Omit jam and replace water with sweet dessert wine.

veggie sides

Roasted Veggies

[Serves 4-6]

1-2 tbsp extra virgin coconut oil
1 pound (16 oz) (450g) fresh vegetables, such as peppers,
Brussels sprouts (bottoms trimmed and halved,) zucchini slices,
cauliflower florets, beet root (peeled and cut into chunks), or
carrot slices
2-3 tbsp extra virgin olive oil
a sprinkle of sea salt
¼ cup (1 oz) (28g) fresh parmesan, grated finely (optional)

If roasting several different types of veggies, be sure they are all roughly the same size pieces. Grease bottom of a dark colored (not glass) roasting pan with a little coconut oil. Using a dark pan helps veggies brown easier and faster. Arrange veggies on pan and bake at 400°F (200°C) for 30-45 minutes until lightly browned and tender. Drizzle with olive oil and sprinkle with sea salt. Add parmesan if desired.

Roasted Asparagus

[Serves 4-6, if you are lucky]

2 large bunches asparagus
2 tbsp extra virgin olive oil
sea salt to taste

On a baking sheet arrange asparagus in a single layer then bake at 400°F (200°C) for 3-5 minutes depending on thickness of the spears. You want them just a little softened, but still stiff as they will continue to cook when out of the oven. Remove and place in a serving dish. Toss with the oil and sprinkle with sea salt to serve.

Roasted Cauliflower with Tahini Sauce

Cauliflower is in the same family as broccoli, kale, cabbage, and collards. It is loaded with antioxidants, anti inflammatories, and digestive protectants which means that not only does it taste fabulous, but it is just as fab for your body, so tuck in!

[Serves 4-6]

1 tbsp extra virgin coconut oil
1 head of cauliflower, broken into florets
3-4 tbsp extra virgin olive oil
1 tsp cumin seeds (optional)
½ tsp chili flakes (optional)

SAUCE
8 tbsp tahini
juice of 2 lemons (4 tbsp)
4 tbsp water
2 small garlic cloves, crushed

Lightly grease bottom of a dark roasting pan with coconut oil and place the cauliflower in a single layer. Bake at 375°F (190°C) for about 20-30 minutes until lightly browned and slightly tender. Add cumin and chili during last 5 minutes, if desired. Remove from the oven and toss in olive oil to coat lightly.

FOR THE SAUCE: Combine all ingredients in a covered jar; shake vigorously until thickened. Add a little water to thin if necessary. This dip can also be used as a salad dressing by adding 2-3 tbsp water.

Warm French Green Beans & Walnuts

[Serves 4]

½ cup (2 oz) (55g) walnut pieces
2 cups (8oz) (225g) French green beans, topped and tailed
2 tbsp extra virgin olive oil
2 tbsp walnut oil
2 tbsp sherry vinegar
3 tbsp chopped chives
sea salt to taste
½ cup (2 oz) (55g) goat or humbodlt fog cheese crumbled

If time allows, soak walnuts for up to 2 hours in water as this removes the bitter taste and ensures easier digestability and greater nutritious benefits. Dry the nuts.

Top and tail the beans. Heat a little water in a covered pan. and when water reaches boiling, put beans in pan and steam for 3-4 minutes. Then remove and rinse in cold water (this keeps them nice and green). Pat dry. Place beans in a serving dish and toss with oils, vinegar, chives, and sea salt to taste. Garnish with crumbled cheese and walnuts.

Joysie Boysie Okra

[Serves 4-6]

2 cups (8 oz) (225g) okra, topped and tailed
3 medium tomatoes, chopped finely
⅓ cup (3 oz) (85g) tomato paste
6 medium garlic cloves, crushed
⅓ cup (1-2 oz) (28-55g) cooked chick peas
1 large handful cilantro, stems removed
juice of 1 large lemon
3 tbsp extra virgin olive oil

Place okra in a covered pot on medium heat and cover and cook for about 10 minutes until softened. Add tomatoes, tomato paste, and garlic and cook 10 more minutes. Add chick peas, lemon juice, and cilantro and cook just until warm. Remove from heat and mix in olive oil. Serve with pita bread.

Zucchini Carpaccio

[Serves 4-6]

8-12 small to medium zucchini
¼ cup (2 fl oz) (55ml) fresh lime juice
⅓ cup (3 fl oz) (85ml) extra virgin olive oil
2 medium garlic cloves, crushed
2 tbsp fresh oregano leaves or 1 tbsp dried oregano
½ red onion, sliced thinly
½ cup (2 oz) (55g) feta cheese, crumbled
¼ cup (2 oz) (55g) sundried tomatoes, chopped finely

Peel zucchini lengthwise with a veggie peeler so that they are in long thin strips. Lay them in a flat dish at least 1 inch deep.

Combine lime juice, olive oil, and garlic in a blender. Pour over the zucchini strips. Toss in oregano and onions.

Marinate in the fridge at least 15 minutes before serving, or up to 3 hours. To serve, garnish with feta cheese and tomatoes.

Quinoa in a Snap

This is a great side dish, main dish, or starving-after-class snack. It also makes plenty to share with friends or keep in the fridge for later. (Sticks to your ribs on the inside, but not on the outside, so eat up!)

[Serves 3-4]

1 cup (5 oz) (145g) quinoa (sprouted if available)
1½ cups (12 fl oz) (375ml) water
3 tbsp extra virgin olive oil
juice of 2 lemons
3 medium garlic cloves, crushed
1 cup (4 oz) (115 g) feta cheese, crumbled
1 carrot, grated
1 small zucchini, grated
1 small cucumber, chopped finely
1 avocado, pitted, peeled and chopped
2 tbsp fresh herbs (mint, basil, oregano, parsley, etc.)
1 cup (1 oz) (28g) fresh baby spinach or arugula, cut finely
(drained canned tuna or sardines can be added if desired)

Rinse quinoa under water to remove bitter outer coating. Bring water to boil. Add quinoa then cover and cook on low for 13-15 minutes, until softened. Turn off heat and let stand for 5 minutes. Place cooked quinoa in a bowl and add the rest of the ingredients. Toss to combine. (Leftovers are great in wraps.)

Cannellini Beans with Tomatoes and Rosemary

[Serves 4]

1½ cups (4-5 oz) (115-140g) cooked cannellini beans*
1 cup (8oz) (225g) grape tomatoes, halved
1 small red onion, chopped finely
1 tsp extra virgin coconut oil
6-8 tbsp chopped large leaf parsley
1 tbsp rosemary, chopped finely
sea salt to taste
1 tsp red chili flakes (optional)

DRESSING
3 tbsp fresh lemon juice
1 large garlic clove, crushed
⅓ cup (3 fl oz) (90ml) extra virgin olive oil

Roast tomatoes, cut side up, in single layer at 325°F (170°C) for 30 minutes.

Place beans, onion, roasted tomatoes and parsley in a serving bowl and toss with dressing. Sprinkle rosemary, sea salt to taste, and chili flakes if desired.

FOR THE DRESSING: Blend lemon juice, garlic, and olive oil until combined.

*To prepare dried beans, cover with at least 4 inches of room temperature water and soak at room temperature for at least 8 hours or overnight. Drain the water and place beans in boiling water to cover and boil for 30-35 minutes until tender. Drain to use.

Lentils in Sherry Vinegar

[Serves 4]

1½ cups (12 oz) (340g) green lentils, sprouted if possible
⅓ cup (3 fl oz) (90ml) extra virgin olive oil
3 tbsp sherry vinegar
2 large garlic cloves, crushed
2 tbsp rosemary, chopped finely (optional)
1 red pepper, chopped finely
½ small red onion, chopped finely
2 cups (3 oz) (85g) arugula or fresh baby spinach
1 cup (4 oz) (115g) feta, crumbled
½ cup (3 oz) (85g) pistachio nuts, chopped finely

Boil 4 cups (32 fl oz) (950ml) of water and add lentils. Simmer until tender for about 7-10 minutes for sprouted lentils, or 25-30 minutes for regular. Remove and drain.

Blend oil, vinegar, and garlic until smooth. Toss in the lentils. Add all the other ingredients to the lentils except for the feta and nuts. When ready to serve toss in nuts and feta and serve room temperature.

NOTE: This mixture makes an excellent stuffing for tomatoes, too.

Eggplant Bombay

[Serves 4]

2 large eggplants
4 tbsp extra virgin coconut oil, warmed
1 tbsp medium curry powder (for less salt, use Frontier brand curry powder)
juice of 1 lime

SAUCE
¾ cup (6 oz) (175g) plain Greek yogurt
1 tbsp fresh mint, chopped finely
2 tbsp fresh cilantro, chopped finely
3 roasted garlic cloves, crushed
sea salt to taste

Slice eggplants in half lengthwise. Score each half in a criss cross pattern across the flesh but not through the skin. Brush cut sides with oil and sprinkle with curry powder. Bake at 375°F (190°C) for about 25-30 minutes until lightly browned and the flesh is soft. Drizzle with lime juice, then top with sauce and garnish with cilantro.

FOR THE SAUCE: Mix together yogurt, mint, most of the cilantro, garlic, and sea salt to taste.

Roasty Potatoes

[Serves 6-8]

6-8 medium (2 lbs) (900g) organic new or Yukon gold potatoes
⅓ cup (3 oz) (85g) butter or extra virgin coconut oil
sea salt

Boil potatoes with skins on for 10-12 minutes until slightly tender. Drain water and let cool. Cut in halves or thirds depending on the size of the potato. Heat butter or oil in a large roasting pan at 375°F (190°C) and when hot, add potatoes and roll to cover. Sprinkle with sea salt and bake for 30-45 minutes until desired crispiness. Serve hot.

Grilled Potatoes with Tarragon & Yogurt

[Serves 4]

6 small (1½ lbs) (675g) Yukon gold or new potatoes
2 tbsp unsalted butter or extra virgin coconut oil
1 cup (8 oz) (225g) plain Greek yogurt
3 tbsp fresh tarragon, chopped finely, or 1 tbsp dried
4 green onions, chopped finely
sea salt and pepper to taste

Bring water to a boil and boil potatoes for about 10-15 minutes until tender. Drain and cut into halves or fourths depending on the size of the potatoes. Place in a dark roasting pan and toss with 1 tbsp butter or oil. Bake at 375°F (190°C) for 20-25 minutes until lightly brown. Remove and toss in yogurt, onions, tarragon and salt and pepper to taste. Serve warm.

Fanned Roasted Potatoes

[Serves 4-6]

6 small (1½ lbs) (675g) Yukon gold or new potatoes
½ cup (3 oz) (55g) unsalted butter or extra virgin coconut oil, melted
1 tsp sea salt, plus salt to coat
2 garlic cloves, crushed

Slide a skewer horizontally through the bottom of one potato, then cut vertically just to the skewer, not through to the bottom of the potato. Remove skewer and repeat with remaining potatoes. Soak potatoes in water for at least 1 hour to remove the starch, causing them to fan out. One hour before serving, pat potatoes dry. Crush salt with the garlic to form a paste and rub into the slits of the potatoes. Roll each potato in melted butter or oil. Sprinkle with a little sea salt and bake for 30-40 minutes at 375°F (190°C) until tender and browned.

Potato Daphinois

My mom's and my grandmother's all time favorite dish!

[Serves 4-6]

1 cup (8 fl oz) (250ml) water
1 cup (4 oz) (115g) mild goat cheese, crumbled
7 medium (2 lb) (900g) Yukon gold (or sweet) potatoes
1 large sweet onion, sliced finely
3 large garlic cloves, crushed
1½ cups (6 oz) (175g) gruyere cheese, grated
½ cup (2 oz) (55g) fresh parmesan, grated
2 tbsp fresh or 2 tsp dried thyme leaves
1 tbsp unsalted butter

Blend water and goat cheese until combined and heat in large pot. Slice potatoes on a mandolin thinly or by hand and add to pot along with 2 crushed garlic cloves. Cover and cook on low 10-15 minutes until tender. Meanwhile, slice onions on a mandolin thinly or by hand. Cook onions in covered saucepan for 5-10 minutes on low until softened.

Grease a 7x11 inch glass pan and rub with 1 crushed garlic clove. Pour half the potato mixture into the pan and cover with half the cheeses and half the thyme. Then top with a layer of onions. Top with the remaining potatoes and top with the rest of the cheese and thyme. Cover the baking dish with foil and bake at 375°F (190°C) for about 30 minutes. Then remove foil and bake another 5-10 minutes until lightly browned and bubbling. Cut into squares and serve hot or warm.

Potato Salad on the Med

This dish will sweep you away to the Mediterranean — plus it packs a wallop of energy and taste. Perfect for a casual summertime get-together.

[Serves 4]

16-20 small (1½ lbs) (675g) new potatoes
½ cup (4 oz) (115g) sun dried tomatoes, drained and chopped
¼ red onion, chopped finely
1 cup (1oz) (28g) fresh basil or baby spinach leaves

DRESSING
juice of 1 lemon
⅓ cup (3 fl oz) (90ml) extra virgin olive oil
1 large garlic clove, crushed
3 tbsp freshly grated parmesan, plus extra for garnish

Boil potatoes for 12-15 minutes until tender. Drain and cut in half. Bake at 375°F (190°C) for 30 minutes until crispy. Toss with tomatoes, onion and basil or spinach.

FOR THE DRESSING: Blend lemon, oil, garlic, and parmesan until creamy and toss with potatoes, tomatoes and spinach.

Serve warm or room temperature, top with shaved parmesan.

Sweet Potato & Goat Cheese Mash

[Serves 4]

3 medium (2 lb) (900g) sweet potatoes
1 cup (4 oz) (115g) goat cheese, crumbled
2 tbsp extra virgin olive oil
1 heaping tbsp rosemary, chopped finely
sea salt to taste

Pierce potatoes with a knife and bake at 375°F (190°C) for 45 minutes until tender. Remove from oven and slip off skins immediately. Place in a bowl and mash with goat cheese, olive oil, sea salt, and rosemary.

This also makes a great appetizer. Roll mashed mixture into balls and sauté in a little extra virgin coconut oil until lightly browned. Serve warm.

Sweet Potato Slammers

Known to sway even the most avowed sweet potato hater!

[Serves 4]

2 medium (2 lb) (900g) sweet potatoes
2 tbsp extra virgin coconut oil
2 tbsp finely chopped fresh sage and rosemary
2 cups (2 oz) (55g) fresh baby spinach leaves
1 sweet onion, cut into chunks
1 cup (4 oz) (115g) Humbodlt fog or Wensleydale cranberry cheese
½ cup (4 fl oz) (125ml) balsamic vinegar

Pierce potatoes and bake at 375°F (190°C) for about 30 minutes until just soft. Remove skins immediately and cut potatoes into 1 inch pieces. Heat oil in a dark roasting pan and toss sweet potato and onion chunks in the oil and place in a single layer and roast at 375°F (190°C) for about 30 minutes until lightly browned.

Remove from oven and toss with spinach and herbs and sprinkle with cheese. Drizzle with reduced vinegar.

REDUCED VINEGAR: Boil vinegar, 1 inch deep in saucepan, on high for 4-5 minutes, until thickened and reduced.

The Great Artichoke Off

Here is the winning recipe of a fierce holiday competition.

[Serves 4]

4 globe artichokes
1 lemon

WINNING SAUCE
juice of 2 lemons
2 large garlic cloves, crushed
¼ tsp sea salt
1 tsp Dijon mustard
½ cup (4 fl oz) (125ml) extra virgin olive oil

Cut the bottom stem even with the base of the artichoke and place in a large pot of boiling water, covering the bottom half of the artichoke. Add juice of 1 lemon and boil covered for about 45 minutes. Drain water, cover and let sit about 10 minutes.

FOR THE SAUCE: Blend juice from two lemons, garlic, salt, and mustard on high until all combined, then gradually add the oil. (This sauce can be done a day ahead and stored at room temperature.)

To get to the heart, after all the leaves have been enjoyed, pull out the pointy cone at the top. Run a knife around the thistley bits and remove with a spoon. Cut up the heart or serve stuffed.

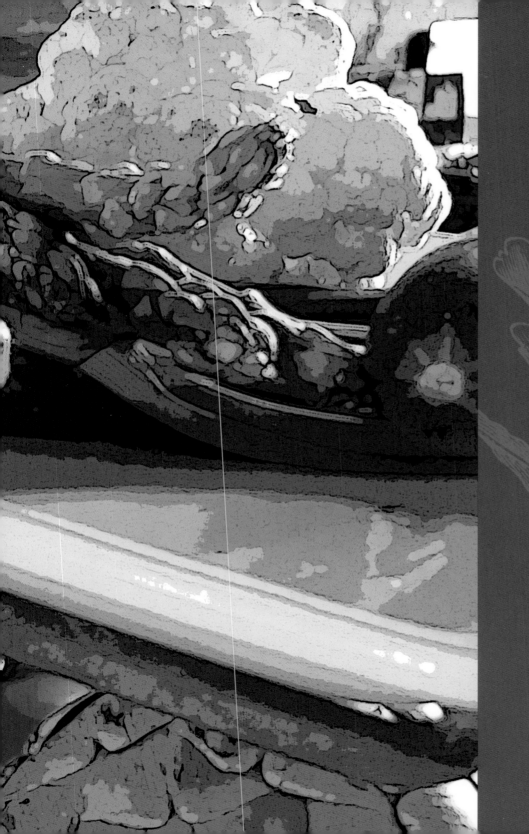

veggie mains

Stuffed Tomatoes

[Serves 4-6]

1 large sweet onion, diced finely
1 cup (5 oz) (145g) quinoa, sprouted if available
1½ cups (12 fl oz) (340ml) water
3 garlic cloves, crushed
2 tbsp fresh oregano leaves or 2 tsp dried
juice of ½ lemon
4 tbsp large leaf parsley, chopped finely
¾ cup (3 oz) (85g) parmesan cheese, finely grated
6-8 small veggie sausages, pre-cooked and crumbled (optional)
6-8 medium - large tomatoes

Place diced onion in a large covered pan on low heat for about 5 minutes until softened. Add quinoa, garlic, and water. Cover and cook an additional 7-10 minutes until the quinoa has softened a bit. (Check halfway through cooking and stir.) Remove from the heat and mix in oregano, lemon, parsley, ½ cup of the cheese, and finely crumbled sausage crumble if using.

Slice off the tops of each tomato and reserve. Hollow out each tomato with a spoon. (Reserve for soups or sauces later.) Fill with the quinoa mixture, mounding it on the top. Sprinkle with cheese. Place them in a baking dish and bake at 375°F (190°C) for about 20-30 minutes just until the tomato is softened and the top is crunchy. This time will depend on how big your tomatoes are. Serve hot or warm.

This mixture is great in peppers or zucchini, too.

Veggie Man Sandwich

A favorite of men and women alike.

[Serves 8]

1 tsp extra virgin coconut oil
1 cup (8 oz) (225g) sweet grape tomatoes, halved
1 red pepper, deseeded and cut into strips
1 yellow pepper, deseeded and cut into strips
1 zucchini, sliced thinly
3 slices red onion
2 tbsp extra virgin olive oil
extra virgin olive oil
1 focaccia round or ciabatta loaf
6-8 tbsp fresh pesto sauce*
1 cup (4 oz) (115g) mozzarella cheese, sliced
4 tbsp freshly grated parmesan cheese
1 handful fresh basil leaves, torn
sea salt, rosemary sprigs or basil leaves

Lightly brush a roasting pan with a little coconut oil and place tomatoes cut side up in a single layer and roast at 325° (170°C) for 30 minutes. Remove and reserve.

Place onions, peppers and zucchini on a piece of parchment paper and roast at 400°F (200°C) for 15-18 minutes until all veggies are softened and slightly browned. Toss in a little olive oil, and reserve.

Cut focaccia or ciabatta loaf in half and remove a bit of the bread from both sides. Spread pesto on both halves and layer the bottom half with strips of grilled pepper, onion, tomatoes, and zucchini. Add mozzarella, grated parmesan, and basil leaves and top with the remaining bread.

Wrap in parchment or foil and bake for 25 minutes. To serve, unwrap, drizzle with olive oil and garnish with rosemary or basil leaves and sea salt. Cut into pie shaped wedges.

*See page 17.

Tastiest Veggie Burgers Ever

[Makes about 6 burgers]

¾ cup (6oz) (170g) sprouted or non-sprouted brown lentils
½ small sweet onion, chopped finely
8 medium (8 oz) (225g) cremini or baby bella mushrooms, sliced
2 large garlic cloves, crushed
½ cup (2 oz) (55g) walnut pieces
1 tsp brown mustard
1 whole grain or sprouted grain English muffin, toasted and torn
1 large egg (can be omitted for vegans)
1 tbsp unfiltered apple cider vinegar

GARNISH
fresh pesto*, goat cheese, arugula, grilled onions

Heat 2 cups (16 fl oz) (250 ml) of water to boiling, add dry lentils and boil 10 minutes, for sprouted ones or 30 for non-sprouted. Drain well and pat dry with paper towels until no moisture remains. While lentils are cooking, sauté onions 5 minutes until soft. Add mushrooms and garlic and cook uncovered 3-5 minutes until soft and no moisture remains.

Place lentils, mushroom/onion mixture, egg, mustard, torn muffins, and walnuts in a food processor and process just until mixture is combined thoroughly. Form mixture into patties for burgers and cook in a frying pan on medium heat with a little oil for about 3-5 minutes per side until browned on both sides. Serve burgers on buns with some fresh pesto, goat cheese, arugula, and grilled onions or whatever you fancy!

* See page 17

NOTE: This recipe makes wonderful meatballs, too.

Tomato Feta Roulade

[Serves 4-6]

1 red onion, chopped finely
3 medium cloves garlic, crushed
7 medium tomatoes
2 tbsp balsamic vinegar
2 tbsp tomato paste
8-10 sheets of filo pastry
8-10 tbsp fresh pesto (See page 17)
¾ cup (3 oz) (85g) feta cheese, crumbled
3-4 tbsp extra virgin coconut or olive oil

Sauté onions in a covered, dry pan on medium low heat until softened, about 5-7 minutes. Uncover and add vinegar, garlic, and tomatoes. Cook, uncovered, until thickened and paste-like, about 15-20 minutes. Mix in tomato paste.

Layer 5 sheets of filo, brushing in between where possible with a little coconut oil. Repeat this with a separate stack of 3 sheets. Place the 5 sheet stack on a piece of baking parchment and spread with the tomato onion mixture, leaving a 1 inch border on all sides. Top with feta cheese. Place the 3-sheet stack of filo on top of this and spread with pesto. Fold the 2 short sides over 1 inch and then roll up along the long end. Place on baking sheet, seam side down. If the roll breaks, roll the remaining 2 sheets of pastry around the outside to enclose. (This can be done ahead and then chilled or frozen, just bring to room temperature before baking.) Brush the top with a little coconut oil and bake at 350°F (180°C) for 30-40 minutes until browned and crisped.

Cool a few minutes before cutting into 1 inch slices. Serve warm or room temperature.

Mushroom & Goat Cheese Parcels

[Makes 12]

9 sheets filo pastry

FILLING
2 shallots, minced
2 large garlic cloves, crushed
1 lb (450 g) cremini mushrooms, sliced
¼ cup (2 fl oz) (55ml) sherry wine vinegar
2 tbsp chopped parsley or rosemary
2 tbsp melted extra virgin coconut oil or olive oil
1 cup (4 oz) (115g) goat cheese, crumbled

GLAZE
½ cup (4 fl oz) (115ml) balsamic vinegar

Sauté shallots, covered on medium heat for 3-5 minutes until softened. Uncover, add garlic, vinegar, rosemary, and mushrooms; increase heat, and sauté for 8-10 more minutes until softened and liquid is evaporated. Place 3 stacks of 3 sheets of filo on cutting board and where possible brush a little oil in between the sheets. Cut into 4 strips along the long end and place 2-3 tbsp of the mushroom mixture at the top of each strip. Sprinkle a little cheese over each mixture and then fold over each into a triangle. Keep folding over into triangles all the way down to the bottom of each pastry strip. Repeat with the other stack and chill until ready to bake. Bake at 375°F (190°C) for about 15-20 minutes until golden brown.

FOR THE GLAZE: Pour vinegar, 1 inch deep, in a pan and boil for about 5 minutes until thick and reduced. Drizzle onto the plates and over the top of the baked pastries.

Asparagus Tart

[Serves 4-6]

I medium (½ lb) (225g) sweet potato, grated medium with skin
½ sweet onion, grated medium
I tsp extra virgin coconut oil
4 cups (4 oz) (115g) fresh baby spinach
½ tsp freshly grated nutmeg
I½ cups (6 oz) (175g) aged gruyere or appenzeller cheese, medium grated
4 large eggs
2 cups (16 oz) (450g) Greek yogurt
½ tsp sea salt
10-13 pieces fresh asparagus

Grease a nonstick 10-inch ovenproof pan and cook onion and potato on medium high until lightly brown and softened. Remove from heat and spread evenly over the bottom of the pan. Add spinach and cover until the spinach is wilted. Top with grated cheese.

In a bowl, or blender, beat eggs, yogurt, salt, and nutmeg until smooth. Pour over the spinach and cheese and top with asparagus spears. Bake in the pan for 12-15 minutes at 350°F (180°C) until just set in the center. Cut into wedges and serve warm or room temperature.

Grilled Vegetable Pesto Risotto

[Serves 4-6]

I tsp extra virgin coconut oil
I cup (7 oz) (225g) arborio rice
2 cups (16 fl oz) (450ml) low sodium vegetable or chicken broth
5 tbsp fresh pesto (See page 17)
3 tbsp extra virgin olive oil
juice of I lemon
I red and I yellow pepper, roasted
I large handful of basil leaves, torn
4-5 green onions, chopped finely
3 tbsp chopped sundried tomatoes
grilled asparagus
½ cup (2 oz) (55g) shaved parmesan cheese
½ cup (2 oz) (55g) pine nuts, lightly toasted

Heat oil in deep pan and sauté rice for a minute. Add stock and bring to a boil before reducing to a low simmer. Simmer covered for 15 minutes until tender and liquid is absorbed, stirring once halfway through.

Remove from heat and stir in olive oil, pesto, juice, peppers, basil, onions, tomatoes, and asparagus.

Sprinkle cheese and pine nuts over the top and garnish with a little basil.

NOTE: This is also delicious with grilled chicken.

Real Men Do Eat Quiche

This recipe lives up to its name! The four men living under my roof devour this quiche – just as long as I don't call them on it.

[Serves 4-6]

PASTRY

¼ cup (2 oz) (55g) cold unsalted butter
¼ cup (2 oz) (55g) cold extra virgin coconut oil
1¼ cups (5 oz) (145g) whole wheat pastry or sprouted flour
3 tbsp cold water
½ tsp sea salt (optional)
¼ cup (1 oz) (28g) parmesan, grated (optional)

FILLING

1 cup (8 fl oz) (250ml) unsweetened almond or whole milk
2 large eggs
1 cup (4 oz) (115g) garlic herb goat or boursin cheese, crumbled
½ cup (2 oz) (55g) feta cheese, crumbled
½ cup (4 oz) (115g) grilled onions or onion marmalade*

Grate butter and oil into the flour. Lightly pulse in food processor or hand mix until crumbly. Add water and, if using, add salt and parmesan. Form dough into a ball. Between 2 pieces of parchment paper, roll to 1 large round, about ¼ inch thick. Remove top sheet of parchment and then turn crust onto pie pan. Peel away remaining parchment and trim edges. Crimp if desired. Prick with a fork and freeze for about 15-20 minutes, or until needed later.

Preheat oven to 375°F (190°C). Blend milk, eggs, and goat or boursin cheese until combined.

First place onions or marmalade in the pastry. Then pour in the eggy cheese mixture. Top with feta cheese. Bake at 375°F (190°C) near the bottom of the oven for 25-30 minutes. until lightly browned and just set in the middle. For mini quiche, place pastry in mini muffin tins and fill with onions, eggy mixture and feta and bake at 375°F (190°C) for 15 minutes near the bottom of the oven.

*ONION MARMALADE

2 medium red onions, sliced thinly
¼ cup (2 fl oz) (60ml) balsamic vinegar
1 tsp coconut sugar
1 tsp dried thyme

FOR THE MARMALADE: Place onions in a covered Dutch oven and cook on low heat until softened, about 10 minutes. Add vinegar, sugar, and thyme. Cover and bake at 350°F (180°C) for about 35-45 minutes until thickened.

NOTE: The onion marmalade can also be used for flan or served in filo baskets or over meat.

Pizza From Scratch

Pizza is great on those nights when we have to eat quickly and sometimes on the run. Mushrooms, onion, and peppers are a favorite with the boys and this is a quick painless way to get some veggies in them. I often double this recipe so I have a spare crust on hand.

CRUST
1 packet active dry yeast
2 cups (8 oz) (225g) whole wheat or sprouted flour
1 cup warm water (8 fl oz) (250ml) (⅓ cup boiling and ⅔ cup room temperature)
½ tsp sea salt, optional
flour for dusting

SAUCE
7 oz (200g) tomato paste
7 oz (200g) diced or crushed tomatoes
2 medium garlic cloves, crushed
1 tsp dried oregano

TOPPINGS
spinach, sliced onions, peppers, mushrooms, fennel, or squash
grated mozzarella, cheddar, parmesan and/or goat cheese

FOR CRUST: Whisk together 1 tbsp of flour with the yeast and ¼ (2 fl oz) (55ml) cup warm water until combined. Stir in 1½ cups (6 oz) (170g) flour and ¾ cup (6 fl oz) (175ml) warm water until combined. Add an additional ½ cup (2 oz) (55g) flour and salt (if using) and stir to combine. Dust hands and dough with a little bit of flour and form dough into a ball. (If it is very sticky, dust again with flour.) Place dough in a bowl and cover with a warm tea towel. Leave to rise for 1 hour or place in the fridge up to 1 day before making pizza.

FOR SAUCE: Blend tomato paste, tomatoes and garlic until smooth then add 2 tsp of oregano.

To make pizza, preheat baking stone or sheet until hot at 450°F (230°C). Dust hands and parchment paper with flour. Place dough ball on paper and roll out to 16-inch round or square for a thin crust. (For thicker crust, roll to 14 inches.) Spread tomato sauce on the crust. Layer with toppings followed by cheese and sprinkle with dried oregano or herbs. Place in the oven near the bottom and bake for 15-20 minutes until bottom is crisp and cheese is lightly browned. Serve warm.

When time is very short, use prepared pizza dough and top with sauce, toppings, and bake as directed.

Roasted Butternut Squash Cornmeal Pizza

1 cornmeal pizza crust (try Vicolo brand, in the freezer section)
½ medium butternut squash
1 small sweet onion, cut into wedges
1 tsp extra virgin coconut oil
1 cup (2 oz) (55g) fresh baby spinach leaves
½ cup (2 oz) (55g) mild goat cheese, crumbled
or parmesan or Swiss gruyere, shaved finely
1 handful warmed walnuts or reserved toasted squash seeds
rosemary or sage leaves to garnish

SAGE PESTO
2 tbsp sherry vinegar
¼ cup (2 fl oz) (55ml) extra virgin olive oil
about 2 oz (1-2 inch piece) (55g) fresh parmesan
½ cup (3 oz) (85g) walnuts, soaked for 2 hours, drained and
dried
2 cups (2 oz) (55g) fresh baby spinach leaves
small handful sage or rosemary leaves

Peel squash with a vegetable peeler and scrape clean. Reserve the seeds to toast. (Toast on a baking sheet about 5 minutes at 350°F (180°C) just until lightly toasted. Toss lightly in a little olive oil and sprinkle with sea salt.) Cut squash into 1-2 inch chunks. Coat dark colored baking dish with oil and place the squash pieces in single layer in the pan. Tuck onion wedges around. Bake at 375°F (190°C) for 30 minutes until lightly browned and softened, then toss with spinach leaves and set aside.

Bake the cornmeal crust at 375°F (190°C) for about 5-7 minutes until lightly toasted, remove, and set aside.

FOR THE PESTO: Place vinegar, olive oil, garlic, and parmesan in a blender and blend on high until combined. Add sage, spinach leaves, and walnuts and pulse on low just until combined, but a little chunky.

Cover the tart bottom with a layer of pesto. Arrange squash mixture over it. Garnish with seeds or nuts and shaved cheese. Cut into wedges or squares to serve.

Tomato Tart

Here's a simple way to showcase those summer tomatoes.
Plus, it can all be done ahead!

[Serves 4-6]

½ tsp extra virgin coconut oil
6 tomatoes, sliced
1 red onion, peeled and cut into wedges
1 large sheet 14 oz (400g) puff pastry

¾ cup (6 oz) (175g) fresh basil pesto*
basil leaves to garnish

Heat oven to 350°F (180°C). Coat the inside of a roasting pan with coconut oil. Place tomato slices in the pan and bake for 30 minutes until slightly shrivelled. Remove and cool before transferring.

Meanwhile, place onions in a covered pan and cook on low for 7-10 minutes until softened and lightly browned. Set aside. Roll out pastry on a piece of baking parchment to ⅛ inch thick and place in the oven on the center rack at 350°F (180°C). Bake 15-18 minutes until lightly browned and crisp. Remove and spread pesto over the pastry. Fill with onions, and then a layer of roasted tomato slices. (This can be assembled several hours in advance and kept at room temperature.) When ready to serve, warm tart in the oven at 350°F (180°C) for 5 minutes, or serve at room temperature. Garnish with fresh basil leaves. Cut into squares to serve.

See page 17.

Lemon Spaghetti with Asparagus & Basil

Only 20 minutes from cupboard to plate.

[Serves 4-6]

juice of 3 lemons
½ cup (4 fl oz) (115ml) extra virgin olive oil
1¼ cups (5 oz) (150g) parmesan cheese, grated finely
1 large garlic clove, crushed
1 box (8 oz) (225g) whole wheat or artichoke spaghetti or fettucini
1 cup of basil leaves, torn
1 large bunch of asparagus, woody ends snapped off
fresh ground pepper

Combine lemon juice, olive oil and garlic in blender. Then add parmesan until thick and creamy. (For best taste, parmesan should be freshly grated.) Set aside.

Cook pasta in boiling salted water for 8-10 minutes or until al dente. Drain thoroughly and return to the pan. Add sauce and asparagus to the pasta, stir, cover, and let the pasta set for 5 minutes to absorb some of the sauce. Finally add basil and fresh ground pepper if desired.

NOTE: Great with shrimp or chicken, too.

Fast Tomato Sauce

[Serves 4-6]

1 jar (24 oz) (680g) whole or diced tomatoes
1 jar (7 oz) (200g) tomato paste
4 large garlic cloves, crushed
3 tbsp fresh oregano leaves or 1½ tbsp dried oregano

Place all ingredients in a blender and blend on low for chunkier sauce or on high for a very smooth sauce. Cook in a uncovered saucepan on medium high for about 15 minutes until boiling and thickened. This can be served straightaway or stored in the fridge for 3 days or freezer for up to 3 months.

Veggie Stack

Perfect for those days when you can't be bothered to turn on the oven.

[Serves 4-6]

2-3 medium zucchini
2 tbsp extra virgin olive oil
½ tsp sea salt

PEPPER SAUCE
1 red pepper, deseeded and roasted
⅔ cup (3 oz) (85g) feta cheese, crumbled
2 medium garlic cloves, crushed
pinch of red pepper flakes
large handful (½ cup) fresh basil leaves
1 cup (7 oz) (200g) tomato paste

1 lb (450g) cremini mushrooms, chopped very finely
2 medium garlic cloves, crushed

Slice zucchini ⅛ inch thick on a mandolin if possible. Rub with olive oil and sea salt and leave for about 20 minutes to soften. Drain and set aside.

Place pepper sauce ingredients in a blender and blend on high until combined and set aside.

Sauté mushrooms on medium high heat until all the liquid has evaporated. Add garlic and set aside.

To assemble, cover the bottom an 8x8 glass pan with half the red pepper sauce. Top with a zucchini layer and then half of the mushroom mixture. Cover this with a zucchini layer, then the rest of the red pepper mixture, another layer of zucchini, and then the rest of the mushroom mixture. Chill. Then 30 minutes before serving bring to room temperature. Cut into squares to serve.

Zucchini Pesto Lasagna

[Serves 4]

juice of 3 lemons
⅓ cup (3 fl oz) (85ml) extra virgin olive oil
4 small zucchini, cut into thick slices and roasted
3 medium garlic cloves, crushed
2 cups (2 oz) (55g) fresh basil leaves
2 cups (2 oz) (55g) fresh baby spinach leaves
2 cups (8 oz) (225g) medium grated parmesan cheese
9 fresh lasagna sheets
1½ cups (6 oz) (170g) mild goat cheese, crumbled

Place ⅓ cup lemon juice, olive oil, zucchini, garlic, basil, spinach and ¼ of the parmesan in a blender in that order. Blend to a paste consistency, adding more lemon juice an olive oil if necessary.

Boil water in a large pan and add lasagna sheets a few at a time. Cook just until softened then remove.

Cover the bottom a 9x11 pan with ⅓ of the pesto, then layer with ⅓ of the pasta; then ⅓ of the pesto. ⅓ of the goat cheese and ⅓ of parmesan; repeat. End with a final layer of pasta and top with remaining goat cheese and parmesan.

Cover with foil and bake at 350°F (180°C) for 20-25 minutes. Uncover and bake for 5 minutes until lightly browned. (Cooked chicken can be added in between the layers if desired for a nonvegetarian main dish.)

Sweet Potato Rosti

[Serves 4-6]

1 large (1 lb) (450g) sweet potato, scrubbed and grated medium
1 large egg, beaten
3-4 tbsp whole wheat or coconut flour
1 tsp cumin seed (optional)
a pinch of red pepper flakes (optional)
2 tbsp extra virgin coconut oil
2 tbsp grated sweet onion

GARNISH
1 avocado, pitted, peeled and diced into small pieces
juice of 1 lime
¼ tsp cumin seed
pinch of red pepper

Mix grated potato with egg and enough of the flour to stick together. Add onion, cumin, and red pepper. Form into little flat patties and lightly grease a non-stick frying pan with oil and heat until hot. Place the patties in the hot pan and cook on one side until crispy then flip. Be sure not to flip too early or they will fall apart.

FOR THE GARNISH: Mix onion, avocado, lime juice, cumin, and pepper.

(This dish can be served warm or room temperature. To rewarm put in oven for 5 minutes at 375°F (190°C) then garnish to serve.)

SWEET POTATOES

Sweet potatoes, another one of nature's superfoods, contain 65% of the minimum daily amount of vitamin C. Sweet potatoes are loaded with vitamin A and potassium and have a dollop of calcium too. They are loaded with antioxidants that can help prevent heart disease and cancer, and bolster your immune system.

Sweet potatoes are a boon to your skin. Beta-carotene combats free radicals which accelerate signs of aging.

Sweet potatoes are like yoga. Eating sweet potatoes replenishes potassium, which is often depleted during stressful periods. The high potassium content also helps alleviate muscle cramps often related to potassium deficiency.

Among root vegetables, sweet potatoes offer the lowest glycemic index, making them an especially good choice for diabetics. (A sweet potato has a glycemic load of only 17 vs. a white potato index of 29.) So these little gems give a gradual rise in blood sugar and help keep you satisfied longer. To maximize the nutritional benefits of sweet potatoes, consume them with a good fat such as coconut oil.

When eaten with the peel, sweet potatoes have more fiber than oatmeal. Much of their healing potential resides in the skin so save time and enjoy more benefits by leaving the peel on!

Sweet Potato & Spinach Slice

[Serves 4-6]

1 small sweet onion, sliced thinly
5 cups (5 oz) (140g) fresh baby spinach
2 garlic cloves, crushed
1 heaping tbsp chopped fresh sage or rosemary leaves
extra virgin coconut oil for greasing
2 large (2 lb) (900g) raw sweet potatoes, sliced ⅛ inch thick lengthwise (I use a mandoline)
1 cup (4 oz) (115g) mild goat cheese, crumbled (optional)
fresh parmesan, shaved with vegetable peeler
toasted pine nuts for garnish
⅓ cup (3 fl oz) (85ml) balsamic vinegar

Sauté onion in a covered pan on low heat until softened about 5-7 minutes. Remove from heat and add spinach, garlic, and herbs. Stir until wilted. Lightly grease the base and sides of 8-inch round springform pan. Place one layer of sweet potatoes (about half) in the bottom of the pan. Next, layer the spinach mixture and dot with goat cheese and top with the remaining potato slices. Cover with foil and when ready to cook, bake covered in the oven for about 30-40 minutes at 375°F (190°C) or until a knife goes in easily. Top with shaved parmesan and pine nuts and drizzle with balsamic reduction. Remove sides of pan and cut into wedges to serve.

For the balsamic drizzle, pour about an inch of vinegar in a saucepan and boil about 4-5 minutes until thickened and reduced. Cool slightly to use.

seafood

THE FISH HAS SOMETHING TO DO WITH IT

When I was young and single and living in London—before I had fully embraced the idea of cooking—I invited a friend to dinner. This event stands out in my memory, one because it was one of the first times I had ever cooked for someone else, and two I learned a humbling lesson. I'd gone to the fishmonger and had chosen a lovely whitefish and let me tell you it was delicious! My friend complemented me and I guess, high on success, I went into great detail about how I had prepared it. She calmly interrupted my self-congratulatory fish tale by saying, "The fish *did* have something to do with it." Of course she was right.

Always start with the best fish you can find. Buy fresh, not frozen, if possible. Avoid fish exposed to mercury. Always take a sniff before buying. If it has a super strong smell, walk away. Never buy old fish.

Leave skin on when possible while cooking as this makes for a moister, tastier meal.

For a look at which seafood to buy or avoid, and to help maintain healthy oceans, check out:. www.monterey-bayaquarium.org/cr/seafoodwatch.

Fish Haters Fish

[Serves 4]

2 very large garlic cloves, crushed
8 slices Ezekiel or whole wheat bread, toasted lightly
4 rounded tbsp extra virgin coconut oil or butter
4 tbsp parsley, thyme, or tarragon leaves (optional)
1½ -2 lbs (675 - 900g) very fresh white fish (halibut, sole)
juice of 2 large lemons

Place all the ingredients except for the fish and lemon juice in a blender and blend until combined.

Place fish in large ovenproof roasting pan and sprinkle with lemon juice. Spread breadcrumb mixture over fish and bake at 375°F (190°C) for 20-30 minutes. Serve hot (and don't mention it is fish to any fish haters!).

Roasted Fresh Fish

[Serves 4-6]

2 cups (16oz) (450g) sweet grape cherry tomatoes, cut in half
extra virgin olive oil for drizzling
sea salt to taste
2 - 2½ lb (900g - 1.1k) firm white fish fillet, such as: grouper, sea bass, or halibut
2 lemons, one sliced and one juiced
4 tbsp fresh thyme leaves, plus thyme sprigs for garnish
10 cups (10 oz) (285g) arugula or fresh baby spinach
3 tbsp extra virgin olive oil
1 large garlic clove, crushed

SAUCE
2 tbsp tahini paste (sesame seed paste)
juice of 1 lemon
1 garlic clove, crushed
water to thin to sauce consistency

Cut tomatoes in half and roast in a 325°F (170°C) oven for 30 minutes. Then drizzle with olive oil and sea salt and set aside.

Lay fish on parchment paper in a roasting pan and coat with juice from one lemon. Place thyme and lemon slices inside the fish. Roast for about 25-30 minutes at 375°F (190°C) until center is opaque. (Don't overcook as fish will continue cooking after it is removed from the oven.)

Remove skin, head, and tail if desired. Lift top half gently, leaving center bone running head to tail of the fish. Remove bones then remove bottom fillet.

FOR THE SAUCE: Mix tahini with garlic and lemon and thin to a sauce consistency with about 4 tbsp of water. (Sauce can be made in advance and chilled until needed.)

TO SERVE: Sauté spinach or arugula in medium heat pan until just wilted. Remove from heat and toss with olive oil and garlic. Place fillets on bed of sautéed spinach. Garnish with tomato and thyme and drizzle with sauce.

Roasted Fish with Fennel, Red Onion & Spinach

[Serves 4]

1 tbsp extra virgin coconut oil or butter
1 large red onion, peeled and quartered
8 large garlic cloves, unpeeled
3 heads of fennel, topped and bulb cut into 2 inch pieces (reserve fennel fronds for garnish)
1 cup (8 fl oz) (250ml) white wine, plus ½ cup (4 fl oz) (125ml)
½ cup (2 oz) (55g) fresh parmesan, grated medium
juice of 1-2 lemons, plus lemon rind strips for garnish
1 - 1½ lbs (450 - 675g) white firm fish (halibut, cod, or bass)
5 cups (5-oz) (145g) fresh baby spinach
2 tbsp extra virgin olive oil

Place oil, onions, garlic, and fennel in roasting pan and roast at 375°F (190°C) for about 30 minutes until lightly browned and softened.

Boil 1 cup of wine on high until reduced by half. Then place in a blender and add ½ the fennel, onion, peeled garlic cloves and parmesan and blend until smooth. Add juice of 1-2 lemons to taste. (This sauce can be done 2-3 days in advance and refrigerated, or up to 3 months, frozen.)

Place fish in roasting pan and sprinkle with ½ cup of wine. Bake at 400°F (200°C) for about 15-18 minutes until the center is opaque.

Heat the sauce, adding enough of the pan juices to thin the sauce to a pouring consistency.

Place the rest of the fennel garlic mixture in a covered pan and heat on low until hot. Remove, add spinach until wilted. Smash 2 peeled roasted garlic cloves into the spinach and drizzle with olive oil. Divide between plates, drizzle a bit of sauce then top with fish and a bit more sauce and garnish with fennel fronds and lemon rind strips.

Fresh Market Fish with Herbed Hollandaise

[Serves 4]

1 tsp extra virgin coconut oil
1 - 1½ lbs (450 - 675g) fresh fish (grouper, sea bass, or salmon)
1 cup (8 fl oz) (225ml) dry, fruity white wine

HOLLANDAISE SAUCE
2 large egg yolks
3 tbsp water
½ tsp Dijon mustard
2 tbsp lemon or lime juice
5 tbsp extra virgin coconut oil
1 handful (½ cup) fresh basil, tarragon, or thyme leaves

Preheat oven to 375°F (190°C) and coat the bottom of a roasting pan with oil. Place fish in roasting pan, top with some thyme sprigs and cover with wine. Bake for about 18-22 minutes for 1 inch thick fish until fish is just firm and opaque inside but not at the flaky stage yet. Add additional time for thicker fish.

While fish is cooking, place egg yolks, water, mustard and lemon juice in a blender and blend on high until combined. Then heat the oil in a pan until melted and very hot. Gradually pour oil into yolk mixture while blender is on low until all incorporated. Pour sauce back in the saucepan and heat just until warm and thickened. Do not let it get too hot or it will separate. Add torn basil leaves. tarragon, or thyme and serve drizzled on or alongside the fish.

Leek & Parmesan Baked Fish

[Serves 4]

2 leeks, sliced finely
1 cup (4 oz) (115g) parmesan, grated finely
4 tbsp fresh lemon juice and rind of 1 lemon, grated finely
1 tbsp extra virgin coconut oil
1 - 1½ lbs (450-675g) fish, such as halibut, cod, or monkfish, 1-2 inches thick in 1 or 2 long fillets
3-4 tbsp extra virgin olive oil

Remove the root portion of the leeks and cut off the top, just where the green seems to split. Wash thoroughly, opening the layers to wash any grit out of the inner layers. Soften leeks in a covered frying pan for about 5 minutes on medium heat and set aside to cool. When leeks have cooled, mix in parmesan, lemon juice, and rind.

Place the fish in a greased baking dish. Cover fish with the leek and parmesan mixture. (If doing ahead, chill until 30 minutes before serving. Then bring to room temperature before baking.) Bake at 375°F (190°C) for 30-35 minutes, until fish is opaque inside, firm to touch and top is lightly browned. Drizzle with a little olive oil and serve hot.

Soles That Are Stuffed

Finally a fish recipe that is easy, not too pricey, and perfect for a night at home or a friendly dinner party. (Sole is easily found in the freezer section if not available fresh. Dover Sole is pricier and more delicate in flavor.)

[Serves 4]

1 shallot, skinned and chopped finely
3 cups (3 oz) (85g) fresh baby spinach
1 tbsp finely grated lemon peel
1 large garlic clove, crushed
½ cup (3 oz) (85g) sundried tomatoes or roasted red peppers, chopped finely
3 tbsp fresh thyme leaves or flat leaf parsley, chopped finely
4 fillets of sole, about 1½ lbs (675g), skin removed
1 tsp extra virgin coconut oil or olive oil for greasing the pan
1 cup (8 fl oz) (250ml) dry, fruity white wine
3-4 tbsp extra virgin olive oil

Place chopped shallot in a large covered dutch oven pan and heat covered on low for 5 minutes until softened. Remove from the heat and add spinach. Sir until wilted. Add lemon rind, garlic, tomatoes, and thyme, and set aside.

Lay fish on a clean surface. Cut each fillet in half lengthwise so they are no more than 2-3 inches wide. Place 1 heaping tablespoon of filling on the end of each fillet and roll into a cylinder shape. You should have 8 cylinders. Stand these with the filling side up around the edges of a greased roasting pan.

Boil wine for 5 minutes to reduce slightly, then drizzle this over the fish and in the bottom of the roasting pan. Bake uncovered at 375°F (190°C) for about 15-20 minutes until the fish is slightly opaque around the edges. Carefully remove the fish from the pan and serve with some of the juices and some good olive oil drizzled over.

Pineapple Salsa Fillets

This salsa is fab on chicken, too

[Serves 4]

1 large avocado, pitted, peeled and chopped finely
juice and zest of 2 limes
1 tbsp ginger, grated finely
2 large cloves of garlic, crushed
½ cup (3 oz) (85g) fresh or frozen and thawed mango pieces,
chopped finely
3 tbsp brown rice vinegar
1 cup (5 oz) (145g) fresh or frozen, thawed pineapple pieces,
chopped finely
1 red pepper, deseeded and chopped finely
½ small red onion, chopped finely
1 small green chili, finely chopped, seeds and membrane removed
3-4 tbsp fresh cilantro leaves, chopped finely
2 tbsp fresh mint leaves, chopped finely
4 pieces of fish such as halibut; cod or tuna can be used

Mix avocado thoroughly with juice of 1 lime. Set aside. In a blender or covered bottle, combine ginger, lime juice, garlic, a couple of mango pieces and vinegar. Blend or shake until combined. Adjust for sweetness and tartness with the mango and lime. Set aside.

In a bowl, mix pineapple, peppers, onion, chili, coriander, mint, and mango. Toss in dressing and gently mix in avocado pieces. Marinate for a couple hours before serving if you can. For the most robust flavor, add the mint and coriander just before serving.

Grill fish or bake at 400°F (200°C) for about 10 minutes for a 1 inch thick piece or about 5 minutes for a thin piece. Top with salsa to serve.

Poached Halibut in Ginger & Orange

To try and entice my father to eat a healthier diet after his heart surgery, I created this recipe. For true fish haters (like my dad), overcook the fish a bit so it takes on a chicken-like consistency. This sauce is also good on chicken if halibut is out of season or you just need to save a bob or two.

[Serves 4]

2 tbsp fresh ginger, grated finely
3 tbsp rice vinegar
4 tbsp extra virgin coconut oil
3 tbsp reduced fresh orange juice (juice of 2 large oranges
boiled and reduced by half)
1 large garlic clove, crushed
4 pieces halibut with skin, about 1½ lbs (675g)
3-4 tbsp finely chopped cilantro

Mix ginger, vinegar, oil, juice, and garlic and marinate fish in this for up to, but no more than, 30 minutes (otherwise the texture of the fish will go mushy and suffer). Heat oven to 375°F 190°C) and place fish single layer in a dish. Reserve the rest of the marinade for the sauce.

Bake for 15-20 minutes depending on the size and thickness of the fillets. You want them to be just opaque inside but not at the flaky stage yet, unless you like the overdone consistency.

Meanwhile, heat the sauce for the fish on high for 5 minutes until slightly reduced. To serve, drizzle fish with sauce and top with cilantro.

Grilled Wild Salmon with Balsamic Glaze

[Serves 4]

½ cup (4 fl oz) (125ml) balsamic vinegar
½ cup (4 fl oz) (125ml) dry fruity white wine
2 tbsp fresh lemon juice
2 tbsp coconut sugar
4 fillets, about 1½ lbs (675g) wild salmon
2 tbsp extra virgin olive oil or coconut oil

Combine vinegar, wine, lemon juice and sugar and boil on high heat uncovered for about 7-10 minutes, until reduced and thickened. Make sure you use a large saucepan so that the mixture is no more than 2 inches deep, otherwise it will not reduce properly. Whisk in the oil and set aside. This sauce can be made up to 2-3 days ahead and left at room temperature.

Marinate fish for up to 30 minutes prior to cooking in the sauce. Bake or barbecue fish for about 5-7 minutes per side on a medium high heat barbecue or at 425°F (220°C) until opaque inside. Drizzle any remaining juice and reheated sauce over salmon to serve.

Mediterranean Salmon Fillet

[Serves 4]

2 red or orange peppers, deseeded and cut into quarters
1 tbsp extra virgin coconut oil for greasing
8 small fillets, about 1½ lbs (675g) wild or organic salmon with skin
4 sprigs of fresh oregano
4 long chive strands (optional)

POACHING LIQUID
1 cup (8 fl oz) (250ml) dry, fruity white wine
juice of 3 limes
1 shallot, chopped finely

SAUCE
2 tbsp very cold olive oil
4-6 tbsp fresh basil leaves, torn

Place peppers in a greased pan and roast at 375°F (190°C) for 15-20 minutes. Remove from the oven (remove any visible skin) and set aside.

Grease the roasting pan a little more if needed and arrange 4 salmon pieces, skin side down in the bottom of the pan. Slice peppers into strips and place with oregano over the fillets. Top each with the remaining 4 fillets, skin side up to cover. If desired, tie a chive around each salmon stack to secure.

Combine poaching liquid ingredients and boil on high for 5 minutes. Drizzle over the fish. Cover roasting pan with foil and bake at 400°F (200°C) for 20-25 minutes until fish is opaque in the middle. Remove juices and boil for 5 minutes then strain. Whisk in cold olive oil to thicken the sauce. Add finely torn basil leaves and serve with fish.

Sock it to You Scallops

[Makes 4]

8 large scallops, dry packed
1 stick lemon grass (optional)
1 red thai chili, deseeded, white membrane removed, and
chopped finely
2 generous tbsp fresh ginger, peeled and grated
2 tbsp extra virgin coconut oil
1 tbsp honey
juice of 2 limes
4 tbsp finely chopped cilantro

For the lemon grass, remove the outer leaves and grate the inner leaves very finely. Then combine with the chili and ginger in a separate bowl and set aside.

Heat some oil in a large frying pan on medium high. Place scallops in hot pan in a single layer, but not touching. Cook 3-4 minutes per side, turning once when they are just lightly browned. Stir in the honey, lime juice, and the chili mixture. Pile on a serving dish.

These can be served warm or cool, but if you chill them in the fridge, remove 30 minutes before hand to ensure the best flavor.

Garnish with cilantro.

Tuna Burger

I once made these for an impromptu meal for a group of fishies and non-fishies and they were scarfed down by all. Make sure the tuna is very fresh, and ask about the mercury level. Never be afraid to quiz your fish provider as he should know and will not mind being asked. In fact he may even think you are very knowledgeable and may try to entice you into helping out behind the counter.

[Serves 4-6]

1½ lbs (675g) fresh, skinless, boned tuna
3 green onions, chopped finely, some tops trimmed
1 tsp red chili flakes
3 rounded tbsp fresh ginger, grated finely
6-8 tbsp cilantro leaves

SAUCE
½ cup (4 fl oz) (125ml) Soy Vay Vary Very Teriyaki Sauce
2 tbsp raw unfiltered honey

Process tuna, onions, chili, ginger, and cilantro in a food processor, until just combined or cut up very finely. (Pulsing ensures you don't overmix.) Shape the mixture into balls or patties and chill.

Mix teriyaki sauce with honey and brush over each burger. Heat a frying pan (or barbecue) and cook the burgers 3-4 minutes each side, brushing with the sauce during cooking. Heat the remainder and use after as sauce with the burgers.

The tuna patties can be served on buns with cucumber slices, tomatoes and lettuce.

Citrus & Cumin Glazed Shrimp

A party hit every time and a snap to throw together. This is an especially wonderful recipe when time is tight!

[Serves 4]

2 tbsp finely grated fresh ginger
2 tbsp rice vinegar
4 tbsp extra virgin coconut oil
3 tbsp reduced fresh orange juice (juice of 2 large oranges, boiled to reduce by half)
1 large garlic clove, crushed
½ tsp red chili flakes to taste
1 tsp cumin seeds
1 lb (10-15 per lb) (450g) raw large colossal shrimp, deveined and shelled
2 tbsp finely chopped cilantro

Mix ginger, vinegar, 3 tbsp oil, juice, red chili and garlic and set aside.

Heat 1 tbsp oil in frying pan on medium high heat and sauté shrimp on both sides just until pink. Sprinkle in cumin seed at the end to warm. Then stir in ginger vinegar mixture to coat. Garnish with cilantro and serve warm or slightly chilled.

Flipping Shrimp

20 thin slices pancetta (nitrate free)
or thin sliced bacon (optional)
1 lb (10-15 per lb) (450g) raw large shrimp, shelled and deveined
1 tbsp extra virgin coconut oil
2 medium garlic cloves, crushed
juice and finely grated rind of 1 lemon
1 tbsp fresh rosemary, chopped finely
½ cup (2 oz) (55g) crumbled blue, feta, or shaved parmesan
cheese

If using pancetta or bacon, wrap 1 slice or ½ a slice of thin bacon around each shrimp and set aside.

Heat oil in a large frying pan and then sauté shrimp for about 3 minutes per side until the pancetta is lightly browned and the shrimp are pink. Remove from the heat and add in the garlic, lemon, and rosemary.

Place shrimp on a platter and sprinkle with desired cheese. These can be served as appetizers or as a main dish, served on a bed of cooked quinoa.

Marinated Feta Herb Shrimp Baskets

[Makes 9 (3-inch) baskets]

1 tbsp extra virgin coconut oil
1 lb (16-20 per pound) (450g) raw shrimp, shelled and deveined
½ tsp cumin seeds

1 large avocado, pitted, peeled and diced finely
juice of 1 lime
juice of 1 lemon
2 medium garlic cloves, crushed
¼ cup (2 fl oz) (55ml) extra virgin olive oil
10 tbsp (1 large handful) fresh basil, torn in small pieces
6-8 tbsp fresh cilantro, chopped finely
1 red chili or ½ red pepper, chopped and deseeded
¼ small red onion chopped finely
1 cup (4 oz) (115 g) feta cheese, crumbled

TORTILLA BASKETS
3 large wheat tortillas (10-12 inch)
1 tsp cumin or fennel seeds (optional)
2 tbsp extra virgin coconut oil, melted

Heat oil in a frying pan. Add shrimp and cumin and stir until shrimp are pink, then set aside.

Toss diced avocado in lime juice to prevent browning and set aside.

Mix lemon juice, garlic, olive oil, basil, cilantro, pepper, and onion in a large bowl and toss in shrimp to coat. Gently fold in feta cheese and avocado until combined and marinate at least 1 hour or up to 1 day in advance.

For the tortilla baskets, brush each tortilla with a little coconut oil and cut each into rounds 2 inches bigger in diameter than the muffin cups you will be using to bake them in. Heat the tortillas for 2 minutes in a 375°F (190°C) oven to make them more pliable and then sprinkle with cumin seeds. Press into muffin cups. Bake for 4-5 minutes at 375°F (190°C) until lightly browned. Remove and cool.

These can be made a day ahead and stored at room temperature. Fill each with the shrimp mixture and garnish with cumin seeds to serve. (Can be assembled 1 hour before serving.)

Avocado & Shrimp Cakes with Mango Chili Sauce

I prepared this recipe for a Heart Healthy benefit and it proved to be as tasty as it is healthy. Good for a quick meal or appetizer.

[Serves 4-6]

½ - 1 red chili, deseeded and chopped finely
or 1 tsp dried chili flakes
⅓ medium red onion
1lb (16-20 per lb) (450 g) peeled, deveined raw shrimp
1½ tbsp fresh ginger, grated finely
6-8 tbsp cilantro leaves
1 large or 2 medium avocados, pitted, peeled and chopped
juice of 1 lime
1½ cups (4 oz) (115g) unsweetened finely shredded coconut
4 tbsp extra virgin coconut oil

SAUCE
1 tbsp extra virgin coconut oil
1 tbsp curry powder
½ cup (3 oz) (85g) frozen mango pieces, thawed
juice of 1 lime

Place chili and red onion in a food processor and pulse until small pieces. Add shrimp, ginger, and cilantro leaves and pulse until combined. Remove and fold in avocado and lime juice. (Do not over mix or it will be mushy.)

Form shrimp mixture into 1-inch balls. Flatten slightly, then roll in coconut. Heat 2 tbsp oil in a large nonstick frying pan. Sauté until browned on one side; then flip and cook until browned on the other side.

Serve warm or room temperature with the sauce.

FOR THE SAUCE, heat oil in a pan and add the curry powder. Cook 1-2 minutes to open the flavor of the curry. Place this in a blender with the mango and blend till combined. Add lime juice to taste.

NOTE: Shrimp cakes can either be prepared and sautéed just before serving, or made ahead and stored chilled. To reheat, place in 375°F (190°C) oven for 7-10 minutes.

Grilled Shrimp with Tomato, Garlic & Goat Cheese

[Serves 4]

6 medium tomatoes, chopped
2 large garlic cloves, crushed
sea salt and a pinch of coconut sugar
1 lb (16-20) (450g) large raw shrimp, peeled and deveined
1 cup (4 oz) (115g) goat cheese, crumbled
4-5 green onions, sliced thinly
1 handful basil, torn
2 tbsp extra virgin olive oil
juice of 1 lemon

Cook tomatoes, sea salt, sugar and garlic in a large sauté pan until soft and reduced to a thick paste. Add shrimp and cook just until shrimp turn pink, about 4-5 minutes.

Sprinkle with the cheese, onions and basil and drizzle with a little olive oil and lemon juice to serve.

Giant Shrimp with Herbed Yogurt Sauce

[Makes 16-20]

5 tbsp fresh basil pesto*
¼ cup (2 oz) (55g) plain Greek yogurt
2 tbsp freshly grated parmesan
1 lb (16-20) (450 g) large, raw shrimp
1 tbsp extra virgin coconut oil
basil leaves to garnish

Mix pesto with yogurt and parmesan and set aside.

Slit shrimp lengthwise at the opposite end of the tail just so they open up a bit on one end. Heat oil in a large frying pan on medium high heat and then place shrimp in a single layer in the pan and cook just until pink. Remove and serve with the tail up.

Serve with some pesto and yogurt sauce and garnish with basil.

This can be served room temperature or slightly chilled, but not straight out of the fridge as the flavors will be muted.

*See page 17.

Rice Paper Rolls

*Perfect for parties! No cooking required! Just set out the ingredients
and let your guests assemble their own meals.
Use whatever veggies you have on hand.*

[Serves 4-6]

1 package rice paper wraps

FILLING OPTIONS
1 bunch green onions, halved and sliced lengthwise
1 red pepper, deseeded and sliced thinly
1 cup blanched snow peas*
1 English cucumber, peeled and sliced into inch long strips
1 avocado, pitted, peeled and chopped
1 mango, chopped finely
cashews, macadamia nuts, or almonds
cooked shrimp, fish, beef, tofu, or chicken

SAUCE
2 large handfuls cilantro leaves and fine stems
1 tbsp tamari or soy sauce
2 tbsp mango juice from diced mango
2 tbsp lime juice
2 tbsp fresh ginger, grated finely
1 large clove garlic, crushed
½ red chili, deseeded and without membrane
2 tbsp extra virgin coconut oil

*To blanch snow peas: cook in hot water for 2 minutes, then rinse
immediately in cold water.

FOR SAUCE: Combine ingredients in a blender; blend till smooth.

TO ASSEMBLE: Soak each rice wrapper in room temperature water in
a pie plate until soft, about 1 minute. Lay wrap flat and place desired
fillings in the center. Drizzle with sauce; fold both ends in to the center, then roll up and enjoy!

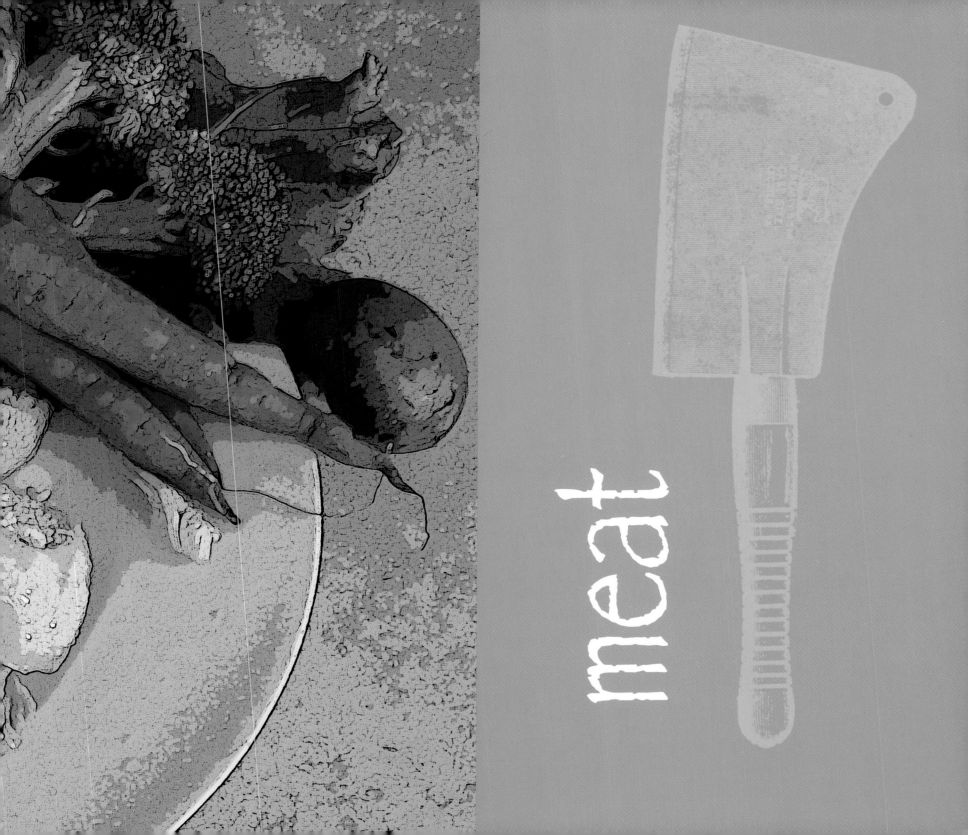

meat

Roast Chicken

[Serves 4-6]

1 fresh whole (3½ - 4½ lbs) (1½ - 2½kg) chicken
1 tbsp sea salt
2 lemons, halved
1 onion, sliced thickly
3-4 sprigs fresh rosemary
3-4 sprigs fresh thyme
1 tbsp unsalted butter

If you can make time and want really crispy skin it is worth it to rub salt on the outside of the chicken and chill for 12-24 hours, uncovered. Remove the chicken from the fridge 30 minutes before cooking. Then remove innards and trim fatty tail flap.

Preheat oven to 350°F (180°C). Place thickly sliced onions in the bottom of a roasting pan or heavy skillet/casserole. This will be the "bed" upon which the chicken roasts. Stuff the inside of the chicken with halved lemons and fresh herbs. Rub the skin with butter then place chicken atop onions. Bake chicken for about 1 hour and 15 minutes. (Chicken is done when leg easily separates from body and juices run clear, not pink or red.)

Let chicken rest 15 minutes before carving. Remove legs and wings and then carve breasts. Drain juices from the pan into a separate container and place in the freezer. This will harden the fat and make it easier to remove. Discard hardened fat and reheat the remaining juices, squeezing the lemons that were inside the chicken into the juice. Serve the chicken in the reheated juice.

Ginger Macadamia Stuffing

Tired of the same old stuffing? This recipe is bound to wake up the taste buds and earn you rave reviews

[Makes 6-8 servings]

4 all butter plain croissants, crumbled
4 tbsp extra virgin coconut oil
1 sweet onion, chopped finely
1 red pepper, deseeded and chopped finely
½ lb (250g) chicken sausage or vegetable sausage, crumbled
1 tsp red chili pepper flakes
2 tbsp finely minced fresh ginger
½ cup (½ oz) (14g) finely cut parsley or cilantro
1 cup (6 oz) (170g) macadamia nuts, chopped finely
1 bunch green onions, diced finely
low sodium chicken or vegetable stock, if baking separately

Bake bread at 325°F (170°C) for about 15-20 minutes until crunchy and lightly browned. Set aside.

Sauté onion in coconut oil in a covered frying pan on medium heat until softened. Mix in red pepper and cook a couple more minutes. Add to this the crumbled sausage, chili, ginger, parsley, nuts, bread, and green onion. Stir until combined.

Bake in a separate dish, moistened with a little stock and bake covered at 375° for about 20-25 minutes until hot and steaming. Then remove cover and bake an additional 15-20 minutes until top is crunchy. Serve hot.

If roasting stuffing inside a bird, add another 30 minutes to the roasting time.

Pot Pies

This is a super quick way to transform leftovers into a knock out meal.

[Serves 4]

1 large sheet (14 oz) (400g) puff pastry
½ large sweet onion, sliced thinly
1 cup (8 fl oz) (250ml) dry white wine
chicken or turkey, 1 thigh and 1 breast
2½ - 3 cups (10-12 oz) (250-340g) raw veggies (broccoli, green
beans, carrots, peas, squash, etc), chopped finely
2 tbsp unsalted butter
2 tbsp white whole wheat or sprouted flour
1 large egg, beaten

Sauté onion in a covered pan on medium until softened, about 5 minutes. Add to other chopped veggies, reserving pan for sauce prep.

Fill a pan with just enough water to cover chicken or turkey pieces. Bring to a boil and cook for about 15-20 minutes until fully cooked. Remove meat (reserve stock for the sauce). Cube cooked meat and set aside.

Melt butter in pan and then add flour. Cook 2 minutes., then gradually add 1 cup of the reserved stock and 1 cup wine into the flour and melted butter mixture, boil while whisking the whole time to prevent lumps. Add more stock if needed to get to a good gravy consistency.

Combine chicken and veggies, then mix with the sauce. Pour into a 9x11 glass baking pan. Roll out pastry to fit top of pan and stretch slightly to cover top completely. Trim any excess.

Brush the top of the pastry with egg. Bake at 350°F (180°C) for 30-45 minutes until top is puffed and golden brown. Cut into squares and serve hot.

Can also be prepared in individual baking dishes. Cut baking time to 25-30 minutes. If preparing ahead, chill the pot pie until ready to bake. Remove from fridge 30 minutes before baking.

Chicken in a Scrunch Pie

Filo is usually fiddley, but not with this recipe. As for the fillings, really any yummy leftovers will do. Voila! An instant dinner that's sure to please.

[Serves 4-6]

10 sheets filo pastry
2 cooked chicken breasts, sliced thinly (leftover chicken works great for this)
½ cup (3 oz) (85g) sundried tomatoes in olive oil, drained; oil reserved
3 cups (5 oz) (145g) fresh baby spinach
1 cup (1 oz) (20g) basil leaves, torn
1 large sweet onion, sliced thinly
2 large garlic cloves, crushed
2 cups (8 oz) (225g) garlic herb or regular goat cheese, crumbled

Place 8 sheets of filo pastry in an ungreased 9x11 baking pan. Roll leftover sheets immediately in plastic and store in fridge or freezer.

Brush a little of the reserved olive oil in between every other sheet in the pan. Gently scrunch pastry along sides. Bake at 375°F (190°C) for about 7 minutes, until just lightly browned. Remove and cool.

Sauté onion in a covered pan on low heat for about 5-7 minutes until soft. Remove from heat and stir in spinach, garlic, basil, chicken, tomato, and 3 tbsp reserved oil from tomatoes.

Sprinkle crumbled cheese over the filo crust. Top with the chicken mixture and scrunch a few filo pieces over the top. Bake at 350°F (180°C) for 10 minutes until heated through and filo is browned. For a non-dairy option, try thickened Tahini sauce in place of the goat cheese.

THICKENED TAHINI SAUCE
6 tbsp tahini
1-2 large garlic cloves, crushed
juice of 1 lemon
1-2 tbsp water.

Shake in a covered container tahini, garlic and lemon until very thick then add enough water till paste-like consistency. Use this in place of the cheese.

NOTE: For a vegetarian option, omit chicken.

Apricot & Brie Stuffed Chicken Breast

Always a favorite!
Summer or winter, this chicken dish gets rave reviews.

[Serves 4-6]

2 cups (10 oz) (285g) raspberries, fresh or frozen, drained
1-2 tbsp coconut sugar
7 fl oz (200ml) port, zinfandel, or cabernet
4 chicken breasts, skinless and boneless
4 fresh apricots or 12 semi-dried apricots
2 medium wedges (about 12 oz) (340g) double or triple cream
brie with rind, cut into ¼ inch slices

Place berries, sugar to taste, and port or wine in a wide bottomed saucepan and boil on high for about 15-20 minutes until thickened and reduced. Strain sauce through a fine sieve to remove berry seeds and reserve.

Cut chicken breasts lengthwise, leaving one side attached so that it opens like a book. Place pieces of apricot and one slice of brie inside each piece of chicken. Fold over to close. Wrap in parchment paper or foil, twisting ends to close and place in a roasting pan.

Bake at 375°F (190°C) for 30 minutes. Unwrap and place one slice of brie on top of each chicken breast and broil for 2-3 minutes, until cheese is melted and lightly browned.

Let stand 5 minutes and then slice each breast into ½. slices. Fan slices on a platter, drizzling reserved chicken juices over the top. Warm the raspberry sauce and drizzle a little sauce over the top. Serve the rest of the sauce alongside.

Sweet Potato Crusted Chicken

[Serves 4]

1 bag (6 oz) (170g) sweet potato chips, unsalted, crushed finely
2 tbsp finely chopped fresh rosemary or thyme leaves
sea salt to taste
whole wheat or coconut flour for dusting
2 large eggs, whisked
2 boneless skinless chicken breasts, halved to make 4 fillets
2-3 tbsp extra virgin coconut oil

Combine crushed chips with herbs and salt. Place flour in one bowl, beaten egg in another, and crushed chips and herbs and sea salt in another bowl. Dust chicken with flour, dip in egg, then roll in crushed chips.

Brush a baking pan with oil and heat in a 400°F (200°C) oven until hot. Lay breasts in single layer on the hot pan. Bake for 10 minutes until browned on the bottoms. Then flip and bake 10 minutes more. Let rest for 5 minutes and serve warm.

Chicken Marsala over Spaghetti Squash

[Serves 4]

1 spaghetti squash
2 boneless skinless chicken breasts, halved, to make 4 fillets
1 tbsp extra virgin coconut oil
8 oz (225g) baby bella or cremini mushrooms, sliced thinly
1½ cups (12 fl oz) (340ml) sweet marsala wine
2 large thyme sprigs, plus extra for garnish
¼ cup (2 oz) (55g) plain Greek yogurt

Cut squash in half and remove seeds and scrape clean. Lay cut side down on a baking sheet and bake at 375°F (190°C) for about 25 minutes, until softened. Using a fork scrape out squash flesh which will come out like pasta tendrils and set aside.

Heat oil in frying pan on medium heat and sauté chicken until lightly browned on both sides. (These will not take long, probably about 3-4 minutes per side.) Remove and keep warm.

Do not wash the pan, but add the mushrooms and sauté quickly on high heat until lightly browned. Add marsala wine and boil for about 3-4 minutes until the liquid is slightly reduced scraping up bits from the bottom of pan. Remove from the heat and mix in thyme and yogurt.

Place cooked squash on platter and toss with a little extra virgin olive oil. Pour some marsala sauce over squash, top with the cooked chicken and top with rest of sauce. Garnish with fresh thyme sprigs.

Chicken "Crackers" with Tomato Coulis

I like these because you can make a large batch and stick them in the freezer. Just defrost later and bake to serve.

[Serves 4-6]

3 cups (3 oz) (85g) fresh baby spinach
½ cup (4 oz) (125g) sun dried tomatoes in olive oil
1 cup (4 oz) (115g) artichoke hearts (I use frozen, defrosted)
1 ¼ cup (5 oz) (140g) boursin cheese or garlic herb goat cheese, crumbled
½ cup (2 oz) (55g) parmesan cheese, grated finely
4 boneless, skinless chicken breasts

Tomato Coulis
24 oz jar (675g) marinara tomato sauce
1 large clove of garlic, crushed
2 tbsp fresh oregano leaves or 1 tbsp dried
¾ - 1 cup (6-8 fl oz) (175-225ml) low sodium chicken stock

Heat spinach 1 minute until wilted in a dry frying pan and then remove and add cheese and sundried tomato and artichoke hearts.

On a 12x12 piece of foil or parchment paper, place chicken breasts and slice each almost all the way through and open like a book. Put the spinach mixture onto one side of each opened chicken breast and fold over to close. Roll each breast lengthwise in the foil or parchment and then twist each end like a Christmas cracker. (These can then be chilled or frozen until ready to cook.)

Place wrapped chicken in a roasting pan, seam side up to keep the juices contained. Bake in a 375°F (190°C) oven for 30 minutes. Let rest 5 minutes before unwrapping. When unwrapping, reserve juices and then slice each crosswise in 1 inch slices. Fan slices on a platter and serve with some juices poured over the slices and some sauce by the side.

For the Sauce
Mix tomato sauce with garlic and oregano and thin with stock to a sauce consistency. This can be frozen or chilled until ready to serve. Heat until bubbling before serving.

Optional Filling: Sage Pesto & Mushrooms

½ cup (1 large handful) fresh sage leaves
2 cups (2 oz) (55g) fresh baby spinach leaves
3 tbsp extra virgin olive oil
2 tbsp sherry vinegar
¼ cup (1 oz) (28g) raw walnuts
1 large garlic clove, crushed
½ cup (2 oz) (55g) asiago or romano cheese, grated
8 baby bella mushrooms, sliced thinly
1 tbsp extra virgin coconut oil or butter

In a blender or food processor, pulse sage and spinach, olive oil, vinegar, walnuts, garlic, and cheese until smooth, but still a little chunky.

Sauté mushrooms in 1 tbsp oil or butter just until softened then remove from heat.

Lay out chicken breast as before and top with sage pesto and mushrooms and fold over and wrap as above. Bake as above and serve with juices from the packets poured over and a little extra of the sage pesto on the side.

Herby Chicken with New Potatoes & Artichokes

[Serves 4-6]

5 large sprigs of rosemary
3 large cloves of garlic, crushed plus 3 extra cloves, unpeeled
½ cup (4 fl oz) (115ml) white wine
3 tbsp fresh oregano leaves or 1½ tbsp dried
4 tbsp white wine vinegar
4 chicken breasts or thighs with skin
12 small new potatoes, halved if on the large side
2 tbsp unsalted butter or extra virgin coconut oil
2 lemons, sliced
1 cup (4 oz) (115g) fresh or frozen, defrosted artichoke hearts

Mix rosemary, garlic, wine, oregano and vinegar. Marinate chicken in this mix for up to one day. (Or not at all, if time is too short!)

Boil potatoes for about 10 minutes. Then drain and toss in butter or oil to coat. Remove chicken from marinade and place in a large roasting pan. Scatter potatoes, lemon slices, and artichokes around the chicken. Pour some of the marinade over and around to cover the bottom of the pan. Bake at 375°F (200°C) uncovered for about 45-60 minutes until golden brown. Serve hot.

Tarragon Chicken & Spinach Lasagna

[Serves 6-8]

3 boned chicken breasts
24 fl oz (675 ml) chicken stock
12 fl oz (340ml) dry white wine
2 tbsp unsalted butter
2 tbsp whole wheat flour
2 tbsp fresh tarragon minced finely, plus extra for garnish
2 cups (8 oz) (225g) gruyere cheese, grated
1 cup (4 oz) (115g) fresh parmesan, grated
½ cup (2 oz) (55g) pancetta (nitrate free)
or bacon, chopped finely (optional)
1 large onion, chopped finely
3 large cloves garlic, crushed
5 cups packed (5 oz) (140 g) fresh baby spinach
3-4 tbsp fresh tarragon, chopped finely or 1 tbsp dried
freshly ground pepper
9 whole wheat or artichoke lasagna sheets

Poach chicken in the stock and wine for 15 minutes; let cool for 1 hour. Remove chicken and reserve stock. Cut chicken into strips and set aside.

Boil stock and wine on high uncovered until reduced by about half. Remove from heat.

Melt butter in a large saucepan and mix in flour. Cook for 2 minutes. Gradually add stock mixture to flour mixture, constantly whisking. Cook on low until slightly thickened. Add ½ the gruyere cheese and ½ the parmesan. Stir until melted.

Sauté pancetta, if using, with onion, and garlic until pancetta is cooked and onion is softened. Remove from heat and add spinach, chicken, tarragon, and pepper.

Boil water and cook lasagna sheets according to packet and set aside. Put a thin layer of sauce on the bottom of a 9x11 inch lasagna pan. Coat lasagna noodles on both sides with sauce. Place one layer of coated noodles in pan, and top with one half of the chicken mixture. Repeat with noodles. and remaining chicken mixture .Top with noodles and remaining sauce and sprinkle with cheeses.

Chill until ready to bake. Remove from fridge 30 minutes prior to baking and bake covered at 375°F (190°C) for 25 minutes. Then uncover and bake 10 more minutes, until browned on top.

Plum Sauce

[Makes about 1 cup]

9 dried pitted plums, about ½ cup (I use organic Made in
Nature, unsulfured plums)
¼ cup (2 fl oz) (55ml) hot water, plus 2 tbsp
1 tbsp ginger, freshly grated
1 tbsp brown rice vinegar
1 tbsp reduced sodium soy or tamari
1 tbsp honey

Pour hot water over plums and let sit about 15 minutes to soften.
Place plums and water and all the other ingredients in a blender
and blend on high until smooth. This is also a great sauce for chicken
or veggies.

Plum & Ginger Duck

[Serves 4-6]

4 duck breasts
4 tbsp plum sauce
1 heaping tbsp minced fresh ginger
2 tbsp tamari or soy sauce
2 tbsp honey
4 spring onions to garnish

Mix the plum sauce, ginger, soy, and honey together and lay the meat
in the marinade and chill for up to 24 hours before cooking or just
1 hour before grilling. Make sure and remove the meat from the
fridge 30 minutes before cooking, drain and save the marinade.

Heat a frying pan until hot then place duck breasts, fat side down,
in the hot frying pan and cook for about 5-7 minutes on medium
high until browned. Reduce heat to medium, flip, and cook another
3 minutes on the other side. Duck should be pink inside and not
all the way cooked through like chicken.

Let rest for 5 minutes before slicing across the breasts to serve.
Meanwhile, heat the reserved marinade and boil for 5 minutes
adding juices from the cooked meat.

Arrange duck slices on a plate and drizzle with sauce and garnish
with spring onions.

This can also be served over rice noodles and steamed vegetables.
Chicken can be used instead of duck but cook until center is cooked
through and not pink.

Turkey Burgers

This is one of my weekday stand-by recipes. and my four guys swear they love these better than beef burgers.

[Makes 4-6 burgers]

1 lb (450 g) ground (preferably) dark turkey meat
4 tbsp finely grated onion
½ cup (2 oz) (55g) grated cheddar cheese
¼ tsp red chili flakes, optional
4 whole wheat or sprouted wheat buns
toppings such as: lettuce, tomato, onion, cheese, avocado, pickles

With your hands, mix turkey, onion, cheese, and chili flakes just until combined. Do not overmix. Form into four or five thick patties.

Heat a roasting pan in 375°F (190°C) oven. Place burgers in hot pan and bake about 5 minutes then turn and bake another 5 minutes until juices run clear. Alternatively, you can sauté in a frying pan or barbecue. Serve on a bun with preferred toppings.

Fig & Sage Stuffed Pork Tenderloin

[Serves 4-6]

2 cups (8 oz) (225g) Black Mission figs, dried
2 cups (16 fl oz) (500ml) Marsala wine
2 shallots or ½ large onion, chopped finely
5 tbsp fresh sage, chopped finely, plus extra leaves for garnish
1 cup (4 oz) (115g) pecan pieces
1 cup apricot stilton cheese or goat cheese, crumbled
3 large garlic cloves
1 low sodium pork tenderloin (nitrate free)
2 tbsp plain Greek yogurt
2 tbsp cold unsalted butter (optional)

Remove stalks from figs and heat in the wine for 15 minutes until soft. Drain and reserve wine. Finely chop figs. Sauté shallots in a covered pan on low heat for 5 minutes until softened. Add figs, sage, pecans, cheese, and garlic and remove from heat.

Cut tenderloin lengthwise, not all the way through, and open like a book. Place filling in center, against the attached long side, up to ½ inch away from open side. Fold over and secure with string.

Heat Dutch oven on the stovetop and place meat in hot pan. Sear meat by cooking 5 minutes on each side. Place Dutch oven, uncovered, in a 375°F (190°C) oven for 20-25 minutes, depending on the desired degree of doneness. (Pork can be a little pink inside.) Place on a platter, tented with foil, to rest 5 minutes before carving. Do not wash baking pan!

FOR THE SAUCE: add reserved wine to the Dutch oven, scraping any bits on the bottom of the pan. Boil until slightly reduced. Remove from heat. Mix in yogurt and whisk in cold butter if desired.

Slice tenderloin into 1 inch slices. Garnish with sauce and sage.

Sweet Potato & Sausage "Cannelloni"

A winner with adults and kids and even sweet potato haters, too!

[Serves 4-6]

1 tbsp extra virgin coconut oil for greasing pans
1 butternut squash, skinned, deseeded, and cubed
3 cups (3 oz) (85g) fresh baby spinach
3 tbsp fresh sage leaves, chopped finely
2 large cloves garlic, crushed
4-5 large sweet potatoes, cut into 1/8 inch long slices
2 cups (8 oz) (225g) goat, gruyere, or provolone cheese, cubed
2 chicken, apple, or maple sausages, cooked (optional)
1 cup (4 oz) (115g) parmesan, freshly grated
1/3 cup (3 fl oz) (85ml) balsamic vinegar

Coat large, dark roasting pan with coconut oil. Place squash in one layer in the pan. Bake at 375°F (190°C) for 25-30 minutes until soft and lightly browned. Remove and toss with spinach and sage to wilt; add garlic and set aside.

Boil water in a deep pan and add sweet potatoes. You may have to do this in 2 batches as they will stick together if crowded. Blanch for 5-7 minutes until tender and flexible. Remove, drain, and set aside.

TO ASSEMBLE: Mix cheese and crumbled sausage with the squash mixture; place 2-3 tbsp of the mixture on the center of each sweet potato slice and fold each end over to cover. Lay in a greased baking pan single layer, seam side down. Grate fresh parmesan over the top and bake at 375°F (190°C) for 15 minutes until hot and cheese is melted. Serve hot or room temperature.

Boil 1 inch balsamic vinegar on high for about 5 minutes until reduced and slightly thickened. Drizzle over baked potato cannelloni.

Meatloaf Mania

A healthy version of one of my mom's favorites.

[Serves 4-6]

1 lb (450g) grass fed ground lean beef
1 large egg
1/2 medium onion, chopped finely
2 slices whole wheat or Ezekiel bread, toasted
2 cups (8 oz) (225g) white sharp cheddar, in 1/4 inch cubes
5 cups (5 oz) (145g) fresh baby spinach
2 tbsp chopped sundried tomatoes
3/4 cup (7 oz) (200g) tomato paste, (salt free, if possible)
1/3 cup (3 oz) (85g) crushed tomatoes

Mix meat, egg, onion, torn pieces of bread, and cheese. Make two loaves, each 2 inches high. Place one on a 2-inch deep roasting pan.

Heat spinach in a dry pan for 2-3 minutes until wilted. Remove from heat and add sundried tomatoes. Place mixture on the first meat loaf. Top with the second loaf.

Combine tomato paste with crushed tomatoes. Spread over the outside of the loaf to cover.

Pour 1 cup of water around the meatloaf and bake at 350°F (180°C), uncovered for 45 minutes. Slice to serve.

If you prefer, this recipe can make four small individual loaves, just reduce baking time by half.

Beef Bourguignon

*Here's a one-pot meal that practically cooks itself,
yet manages to exude an aura of glamour!!*

[Serves 4-6]

1 tbsp extra virgin coconut oil
1½ lbs (680g) grass fed stewing beef, cut into 1-2 inch pieces
pinch of sea salt
2 medium onions, cut into wedges
8 oz (225g) cremini mushrooms, halved
3 large garlic cloves, crushed
2 cups (16 fl oz) (500ml) good red wine
3 tbsp fresh thyme leaves, or 2 tbsp dried
2 tbsp tomato paste
1 cup (8 fl oz) (250ml) water
4 scrubbed medium new potatoes or jerusalem artichokes
quartered
1 sheet (14 oz) (400g) puff pastry (optional)

Heat oil in Dutch oven. Dry beef with paper towels and then place in hot pan, uncovered. Sear on one side, without moving until browned, 4-5 minutes. Flip and sear other side.

Add onions and cover and cook on medium for about 5 minutes, until they are softened. Add mushrooms, garlic, wine, thyme, and tomato paste. Cover Dutch oven and cook at 325°F (170°C) for 1½ hours. Check halfway and add potatoes or artichokes and a little water if it seems too dry.

To make pastry "hats," line baking sheet with parchment paper. Roll pastry a bit, then cut four, 4-inch rounds. Place on baking sheet and bake at 350°F (180°C) for about 15-20 minutes until lightly browned and puffed. Put a pastry "hat" on each serving of beef.

Tenderloin Tantalizers

[Serves 4-6]

1½ lb (675g) beef tenderloin fillet, grass fed if possible
2 tbsp extra virgin coconut oil
juice of ½ lime
3 tbsp thai red or green curry paste
1 tbsp coconut sugar
1 cup (8 fl oz) (250ml) coconut milk
2 grilled red peppers, cut into wedges
1 grilled onion, cut into wedges
1 handful cilantro, chopped finely to garnish
½ cup (3 oz) (85g) crushed macadamia nuts

Cut the fillet lengthwise into 2 long pieces. Leave at room temperature for at least 2 hours. Then sauté on medium high heat in a frying pan until seared on all sides and medium rare, about 5-7 minutes per side.

Heat oil and curry paste for 3 minutes on medium heat. Then add sugar and coconut milk and boil the sauce for 5-10 minutes until thickened. Add lime juice and set aside.

Let meat rest for 5 minutes, then cut crosswise into thin strips. Place meat slices on wooden skewers with red pepper and onion on either side of the meat. Drizzle with the sauce and let the skewers marinate in the sauce for at least 15-20 minutes before serving.

Garnish with freshly chopped cilantro and crushed macadamia nuts.

Best Beef Ever

If I promise to make this dish for our good friends, my family receives a fab ski weekend in return!
(Yes, I'm the crazy lady trying to board the plane with a piece of meat.)

[Serves 4-6]

1 center cut*, 1½ lb (675g) trimmed beef tenderloin, grass fed if possible

MARINADE
2 large garlic cloves, crushed
1 cup (8 fl oz) (250ml) Soy Vay Very Very Teriyaki Sauce
3 tbsp freshly squeezed orange juice
3 tbsp honey

If tenderloin is 5-6 inches or more in diameter, cut lengthwise into two long pieces. Put all the marinade ingredients in a sealable plastic bag and place the beef in this for a minimum of 2 hours at room temperature or chill overnight. Make sure to bring the beef to room temperature before cooking (out of the fridge for at least 1 hour). Then remove meat from marinade and reserve marinade for sauce.

Preheat oven to 400°F (200°C) and place roasting pan in the oven to heat. Place meat in hot pan and sear, about 10-13 minutes per side. (Or sauté on medium high heat in a frying pan until seared on all sides and medium rare, about 5-7 minutes per side.)

Meanwhile, boil reserved marinade for about 8-10 minutes on high, until thickened. Watch carefully to avoid burning sauce.

Remove meat from oven and let rest for about 5 minutes. Cut beef into thin slices. Add meat juices to the sauce. Drizzle over the meat.

*The center cut is easier to cook uniformly when it's the same in diameter. Just reserve floppy bits for another dish.

Lamb Filo Parcels or Strudel

[Serves 4-6]

1 lb (450g) leg of lamb or beef sirloin
(grass fed if possible), diced
1 tbsp extra virgin coconut oil
1 medium onion, chopped finely
3 garlic cloves, crushed
2 tsp of each ground coriander and ground cumin
⅓ cup (1½ oz) (42g) pine nuts
¼ cup (1 oz) (28g) raisins
2 red peppers, halved and deseeded
5 cups (5 oz) (145g) fresh baby spinach
3 tbsp tomato paste
8 sheets filo pastry
olive oil for brushing

Heat oil in pan and brown meat on medium heat. Add onion, garlic, cumin, and coriander. Cover and reduce heat to low. Cook for about 45 minutes, until meat is tender. Add pine nuts and raisins. Cook about 3-5 minutes, uncovered, until liquid has evaporated a bit.

While meat is cooking, place peppers in a roasting pan, cut side down, in 400°F (200°C) oven. Cook for about 10-15 minutes until softened. Remove as much of the papery skin as possible then add to a blender with the tomato paste. Pulse until just combined but chunky. Set aside.

Sauté spinach in a dry pan 1- 2 minutes until wilted then set aside.

Place 8 sheets of filo on a parchment lined baking sheet and brush oil between every 2 sheets. Place meat along the long end of the pastry then top with spinach mixture and then pepper mixture.

Fold the short sides in about an inch, then roll from the long end, ending with seam side down. Bake for 25-30 minutes at 375°F (190°C) on the middle rack of the oven until lightly browned. Cut into 2 inch slices. Serve hot or warm.

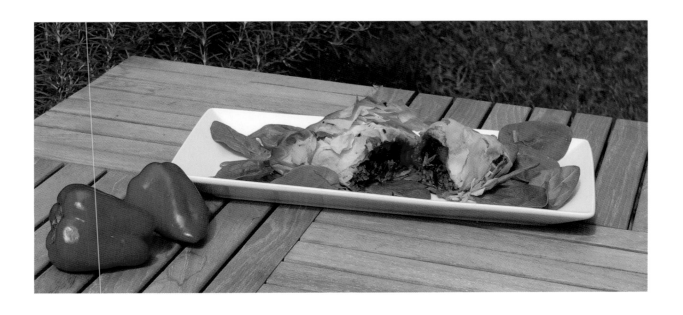

POMEGRANATES

The pomegranate, a sweet fruit with tart undertones, is one of the world's oldest fruits. Records of the fruit date back to 100 B.C. Some Jewish scholars believe the pomegranate, not the apple, was the forbidden fruit in the garden of Eden.

The antioxidant potential of the pomegranate is thought to be up to three times higher than that of green tea and red wine. Rich in heart healthy antioxidants, pomegranates also help keep platelets from clumping together to form dangerous blood clots.

An easy way to extract seeds and juices without diluting the punch of the pomegranate, is to cut the fruit in half and place in a plastic bag, zip shut, and then from the outside work the seeds out and away from the white pith….you get seeds, juices, and no mess with all the punchy flavor and nutrition in tact.

Pizzas with Pizzazz

[Serves 4]

1 small onion, chopped finely
½ lb (8 oz) (225g) lamb, dark turkey, or ground beef
1 large garlic clove, crushed
1 tsp cumin seed
½ tsp ground cinnamon
6 whole wheat pita rounds, or 4 naan breads
1 tbsp extra virgin olive oil
1 cup (8 oz) (225g) hummus (see page 18)
½ cup (2 oz) (55g) pine nuts
1 cup (1 oz) (128g) flat leaf parsley, chopped finely
1 cup (4 oz) (115g) feta cheese, crumbled
½ cup (2 oz) (55g) pomegranate seeds or dried cranberries
lemon wedges to garnish

Heat a skillet or Dutch oven on low heat and add onions. Cover and cook for 5 minutes until softened. Then add meat, garlic, cumin seeds and cook 4-5 minutes until browned. Stir in cinnamon.

Toast pitas or naans at 375°F (190°C) for 4-5 minutes until lightly crisped and remove from oven. Brush with a little oil and spread each with hummus. Next layer the meat mixture, followed with pine nuts, parsley, feta and pomegranate seeds or cranberries. Place in oven for additional 4-5 minutes until warmed through. Serve with lemon wedges.

sweets

A WORD ABOUT SUGAR

Sugar in its natural state, within fruits and vegetables, can be a nutritious part of our diets because it is combined with fiber, vitamins, minerals, and enzymes which help prevent insulin spikes. However, when sugar is extracted from its natural state and refined it loses its beneficial properties.

Too much sugar robs the body of important minerals needed for thinking, coordination, and memory. Eating a diet high in sugar and simple carbs causes us to produce increased levels of insulin which prompts our bodies to store fat. Over time, higher blood sugar and insulin levels can lead to insulin resistance or Type 2 Diabetes. Insulin resistance has become the health crisis of this century. This condition takes its toll on the body and can lead to depression, premature skin aging, high blood pressure, heart disease, cancer, Alzheimers, and Parkinsons.

The following recipes deliver a delicious remedy for sweet cravings without relying on refined sugar. You'll be amazed at how rich and decadent desserts can be with less sugar and even a few veggies (!) blended in.

Macadamia, Coconut & Lime Cookies

[Makes 9, 3-inch cookies]

½ cup (3 oz) (85g) raw unsalted macadamia nuts, finely ground
2 tbsp extra virgin coconut oil
4 tbsp coconut flour
3 tbsp coconut sugar
1½ tsp ground ginger
1 tbsp fresh lime juice
2 tbsp melted white chocolate (optional)

Mix all ingredients together and form dough into a long log. Chill 30 minutes.

Line baking sheet with parchment paper. Slice chilled dough into rounds and place on lined baking sheet. Bake at 350°F (180°C) for 7-8 minutes until lightly browned. Drizzle with white chocolate if desired.

Sunflower Power Balls

[Makes about a baker's dozen]

½ cup (1½ oz) (42g) oat flour*
¾ cup (6oz) (170g) unsweetened sunflower seed butter
2 tbsp coconut sugar
1 tbsp vanilla bean paste
⅓ cup (1¼ oz) (35g) mini dark chocolate pieces (optional)

Mix sugar and oil until combined. Add vanilla and sunflower butter and combine thoroughly. Mix in oat flour and then chocolate pieces if using.

Roll into 2-inch balls and place on baking parchment paper lined baking sheet. With a fork, press lightly in a criss cross pattern on the top of each cookie until flattened slightly. Bake at 350°F (180°C) for 7-8 minutes until lightly browned. Leave to cool on baking sheet before removing.

*To make your own oat flour, simply grind 1 cup (4 oz) (115g) old fashioned oats in a blender until fine. Makes 1¼ cup of oat flour. Excess oat flour can be stored at room temperature for future use.

Dark Chocolate Shreddie Treats

A sweet, energy-boosting snack that doesn't contain any extra sugar and needs no baking so it comes together in a snap. (Keep some in the freezer when you need an extra boost.)

[Makes 12, mini-muffin sized treats]

3½ oz (100g) 70-75% dark chocolate
1 tbsp extra virgin coconut oil
1 tbsp unsweetened almond butter
1½ cups (3 oz) (85g) multi grain square cereal (I use Cascadian Farms) or Ezekiel cereal, crushed fairly finely
2 tbsp raisins (optional)
12 mini muffin liners

Melt chocolate, oil, and almond butter together. Mix in cereal (and raisins if using) until well coated. Drop mixture on parchment lined baking sheet. Cover with a second sheet of parchment and chill to set. Serve chilled or room temperature.

Chocolate Almond Cookies

[Makes 10-12]

¼ cup (2½ oz) (75g) 70-75% dark chocolate
2 extra large egg whites
¼ cup (1¼ oz) (35g) coconut sugar
1 tbsp vanilla bean paste
1 cup (4 oz) (115g) blanched almond flour*
2 tbsp (25g) melted white chocolate (optional)

In a small pan, heat the dark chocolate on low until just melted. Remove and set aside.

Mix egg whites with the sugar and vanilla until combined. Mix in almond flour until thoroughly combined. Stir in melted dark chocolate.

Line a baking sheet with parchment and drop tablespoon-size dollops onto the sheet. Bake at 350°F (180°C) for 7 minutes. Slide parchment paper off baking pan to cool. Drizzle with white chocolate.

To make your own almond flour, simply grind about ¾ cup of whole blanched almonds in a blender to make 1 cup almond flour.

Good For You Snickerdoodles

[Makes about a dozen 3-inch cookies]

½ cup (3 oz) (85g) extra virgin coconut oil
2 tbsp coconut sugar
2 tsp ground cinnamon (Ceylon if you can get it)
2 tsp vanilla bean paste
1 cup (4 oz) (115g) whole wheat pastry or sprouted flour

Cream oil and sugar together until thoroughly combined. Mix in the cinnamon and vanilla. Add flour. Using your hands, combine and form into a ball. (If the mixture is a little loose add a little more flour.)

Place the dough ball between two sheets unwaxed parchment paper and roll out about ½ inch thick. Remove the top parchment paper and using cookie cutters (or the top of a glass) cut into rounds. Separate gently about 1 inch apart. (Alternatively you can form dough into 1 inch balls and then place on baking parchment and squash with palm of hand to flatten slightly.)

Slide the parchment paper onto a baking sheet and bake at 350°F (180°C) for 7-9 minutes just until firm and cookies are lightly cracking on top. Leave on baking sheet to cool. For crunchier cookies leave in the oven 10-12 minutes.

Almond Full of Joy Bites

These fit the bill when I am having a choccie craving but want something that won't tip the scales. A snap to make, and good enough to give out as gifts, too.

[Makes 14]

FILLING
1 cup (5 oz) (145g) unsweetened creamy almond butter
1 tbsp extra virgin coconut oil
1 tbsp coconut sugar
1 tbsp vanilla bean paste

SHELLS
(9 oz) (250g) 70-75% dark chocolate
2 tbsp extra virgin coconut oil
1 tbsp vanilla bean paste

Mix filling ingredients together. Scoop into teaspoon sized balls and flatten slightly.

Melt chocolate with oil. Stir in vanilla. Pour to cover base of small paper candy liners or mini muffin cups. Chill until firm.

When firm, place filling in each. Pour chocolate mixture to cover. Chill until firm. If using mini muffin tins, freeze briefly before removing from tin.

Cream Cheese Marbled Dark Chocolate Brownies

These are "hands down" my boys' favorites!

[Makes 12]

4 oz (115g) dark chocolate (70 -75%)
3 tbsp extra virgin coconut oil
⅓ cup (2 oz) (55g) coconut sugar
2 large organic eggs
1 tsp vanilla bean paste
½ cup (2 oz) (55g) blanched almond flour*
½ tsp baking powder

4 oz (115g) cream cheese
1 large egg
2½ tbsp coconut sugar
1 tbsp ground almond flour
1 tsp vanilla bean paste

1 oz (28g) dark chocolate, melted to drizzle (optional)

Melt the chocolate with oil on low and set aside. Mix eggs, oil, sugar, and vanilla until thoroughly combined. Add chocolate mixture and blend thoroughly. Add almond flour and baking powder and stir just until combined. Pour into a lightly greased 8x8 inch glass baking pan.

In a separate bowl, mix cream cheese, egg, sugar, flour and vanilla bean paste. Pour over the chocolate mixture in the pan. With a knife, gently swirl to marble.

Bake at 350°F (180°C) for 13-15 minutes until set. Cool before cutting. Melt a little extra dark chocolate to drizzle over the brownies, if desired.

To make your own almond flour, simply grind about ¾ cup of whole blanched almonds in a blender to make 1 cup almond flour. Excess almond flour can be stored in the freezer for future use.

Chocolate Bread Pudding with Crème Anglaise

Here's a chocolate bread pudding that's healthy too! Who would guess a yummy slice is loaded with protein, vitamins and minerals.

[Serves 6-8]

7 oz (200g) dark chocolate (70-75%)
2 tbsp extra virgin coconut oil
3 large eggs
1 tbsp vanilla bean paste
2 tbsp coconut sugar
1¾ cups (14 fl oz) (400ml) unsweetened almond or dairy milk

5 slices whole wheat or sprouted wheat bread, cut into halves diagonally

CRÈME ANGLAISE
2 large eggs plus 2 large egg yolks
1 tbsp vanilla bean paste
2 tbsp whole wheat pastry or sprouted flour
1 tbsp coconut sugar
1½ cup (12 fl oz) (375ml) unsweetened almond or dairy milk

Melt chocolate with oil. Mix together eggs, vanilla, sugar, and milk. Blend in chocolate mixture. Pour one third of the mixture in the bottom of a 9x9 baking dish. Layer with half of the bread. Pour another third of the mixture in dish. Layer remaining bread over, pressing down to cover. Pour remaining chocolate on top and chill overnight to absorb. Bake at 350°F (180°C) for 25-30 minutes until set.

CREME ANGLAISE: Combine eggs, yolks, vanilla bean paste, flour, and sugar in a blender. Heat milk until warm, then combine with egg mixture. Pour into saucepan and heat gently until steaming and thickened. Serve warm or room temperature with the pudding.

Warm Chocolate & Almond Tart

When only a deep dark choccie treat will do!

CRUST

⅔ cup (2½ oz) (70g) whole wheat pastry or sprouted flour
3 tbsp extra virgin coconut oil
3 tbsp coconut sugar
2 tbsp cold water
½ tsp cinnamon (optional)

FILLING

1 cup (8 fl oz) (250ml) water
¾ cup (4 oz) (115g) whole blanched almonds
½ cup (2½ oz) (70g) coconut sugar
4 large eggs
2 tbsp unsweetened cocoa powder
3½ oz (100 g) dark chocolate (70-75%), melted
3-4 tbsp all fruit raspberry jam (optional)
fresh raspberries for garnish if desired

Soak almonds for 8 hours in water; drain and rinse.

CRUST: Mix all crust ingredients, except water, until combined. Add water and mix together until dough forms. Place between 2 sheets unwaxed parchment paper and roll to the thickness of leather. Drape over 8- or 9-inch round, springform pan. Press into the pan and trim edges.

FILLING:
Combine water and almonds in a blender and blend on high until thoroughly combined. Add rest of ingredients and blend on high until smooth. If using jam, brush over the bottom of the crust and then pour the filling into the case and bake at 350°F (180°C) for 20-25 minutes until set, but still wobbly in the center.

Let stand in the pan to cool.

Raspberry Bakewell Tarts aka Fairy Cakes

[Makes 6 tarts]

1 cup (4 oz) (115g) blanched almond flour*
¼ cup (1¼ oz) (35g) coconut sugar
2 large eggs
¼ cup (1½ oz) (42g) extra virgin coconut oil
6 fresh raspberries
2 tbsp flaked raw almonds
2 tbsp all fruit raspberry jam
organic powdered sugar for dusting if desired

Mix almond flour, coconut sugar, eggs and oil until thoroughly combined. Pour into lightly greased muffin tins. Spread dollop of jam over each and sprinkle with almonds. Press a fresh raspberry in each center. Bake at 350°F (180°C) for about 13 minutes, until set. Sprinkle with powdered sugar if desired.

To make your own almond flour, simply grind about ¾ cup of whole blanched almonds in a blender to make 1 cup almond flour.

Apple Pie Bars

Here is a versatile dessert bar that's great to pack in lunches or serve as a dinner party desserts.

[Makes 6-8]

CRUST & TOPPING
1 cup (4 oz) (115g) old fashioned oats
1 cup (4 oz) (115g) whole wheat pastry or sprouted flour
1½ cups (6 oz) (175g) walnut pieces
⅓ cup (2 oz) (55g) extra virgin coconut oil
⅓ cup (2½ oz) (70g) organic coconut sugar
2 tsp ground cinnamon
2 tbsp vanilla paste

APPLE FILLING
4 crisp (gala, honeycrisp, fuji) organic apples
1 tbsp extra virgin coconut oil
1 tsp cinnamon
¾ cup (3 oz) (85g) raisins

CRUST & TOPPING: Combine all ingredients by hand or in a food processor until clumps form. Press half the mixture into a 9x11 pan, reserving other half for topping. Bake at 350°F (180°C) for about 20 minutes until lightly brown. Set aside.

FILLING: Core, but do not peel apples. Slice thinly. Cook apple slices in coconut oil in a covered pan on medium until softened. Add cinnamon and raisins.

To assemble, spoon apple mixture onto the baked crust and then sprinkle rest of the walnut mixture over as topping. Bake at 350°F (180°C) for 25-30 minutes or until streusel mixture is lightly brown. Serve warm or room temperature.

Wild Blueberry Goat Cheese Bites

[Makes 9-12]

2 tbsp extra virgin coconut oil
4 filo pastry sheets
1 tsp coconut sugar
1 tbsp lemon juice
1 tbsp organic powdered sugar
1 tbsp water
2 cups (8 oz) (225g) mild goat cheese, crumbled
1 tbsp vanilla bean paste
1 cup (5 oz) (145g) blueberries
3 tbsp all fruit blueberry jam

Brush oil between filo sheets where possible and sprinkle lightly with sugar. Cut into 3 strips and then across into fours so that you have 12 squares. (You want the squares to be slightly bigger than the holes in your muffin tins.)

Place pastry squares in an ungreased muffin tin and bake at 375°F (190°C) for about 5-7 minutes just until lightly browned. Remove and cool.

In a bowl, mix powdered sugar, lemon juice, and water until it forms a loose paste. Add goat cheese and vanilla bean paste and stir until combined.

In a separate bowl, combine blueberries with the jam and set aside. To assemble, place some of the goat cheese mixture into the filo pastry baskets and top with some of the blueberry mixture. Serve room temperature.

Lemon Lavender Tarts

[Makes 6]

6 tbsp fresh lemon juice
2 large eggs
6 tbsp coconut sugar
¾ cup (6 fl oz) (175ml) unsweetened almond or coconut milk
½ tsp vanilla bean paste
2½ tbsp melted extra virgin coconut oil
2 tbsp blanched almond flour*
pinch of dried lavender

Blend lemon juice, eggs, sugar, milk, vanilla, oil and almond flour on high until thoroughly combined. Pour mixture into small (2-inch diameter) ramekins, filling about ¾ full. Sprinkle with a bit of dried lavender.

Place ramekins in a roasting pan. Carefully fill pan with boiling water until the water reaches half way up the ramekins. Bake at 350°F (180°C) for 18-20 minutes until just set. Serve at room temperature.

*To make your own almond flour, simply grind about ¾ cup of whole blanched almonds in a blender to make 1 cup almond flour. Excess almond flour can be stored in the freezer for future use.

Carrot Cake

[Makes 1 two-layer cake]

1 cup (4 oz) (115g) chopped walnuts
1 cup (6 oz) (170g) extra virgin coconut oil
1 cup (5 oz) (140g) coconut sugar
4 large eggs
2 cups (10 oz) (280g) finely grated carrot
1 cup (8 oz) (225g) finely chopped, juiced fresh pineapple
2 cups (8 oz) (225g) whole wheat or sprouted flour
2 tsp cinnamon powder
2 tsp baking powder
2 tsp vanilla bean paste
coconut oil for greasing pans

Frosting

2 pkgs (16 oz) (450g) cream cheese
1/4 cup (1 1/2 oz) (42 g) extra virgin coconut oil
12 large pitted dates, or 1/3 cup (1 1/2 oz) (42g) coconut sugar
2 tbsp vanilla bean paste

Soak walnuts in water for 2 hours. Drain and pat dry.

Combine oil and sugar. Add eggs and mix thoroughly. Add pineapple, carrots, vanilla, and walnuts. Mix until combined.

In a separate bowl, mix flour, baking powder, and cinnamon. Add this to the carrot/egg mixture and mix until just combined. (Don't overmix!) Pour into two 8-inch greased cake pans. Bake at 375°F (190°C) for about 15-20 minutes until cake springs back when touched. Remove from oven and let stand 5 minutes. Remove from pans and cool before frosting.

FROSTING: Place dates in a blender; add cream cheese, coconut oil, and vanilla. Blend on high until smooth. Frost between layers and on the very top of the cake.

Chocolate Cake 2 Beet

[Makes 1 two-layer cake, 12-16 servings]

1/2 cup (3 oz) (85g) extra virgin coconut oil
8 3/4 oz (250g) dark chocolate (70-75%)
3 large eggs
1 cup (5 oz) (140g) coconut sugar
1 cup (8 fl oz) (250ml) unsweetened almond or coconut milk
2 tbsp vanilla bean paste
1/2 cup (2 oz) (55g) raw beets, peeled, grated, (squeezed dry)
3/4 cup (3 oz) (85g) whole wheat pastry or sprouted flour
1/2 cup (2 oz) (55g) almond flour
1 tsp baking powder
coconut oil and cocoa powder for dusting pans

Frosting

9 1/2 (300g) dark chocolate (70%-75%)
1 cup (8 oz) (225g) plain Greek yogurt
1/2 cup (2 1/2 oz) (70g) coconut sugar
2 tbsp vanilla bean paste
3/4 cup (6 fl oz) (170ml) unsweetened almond or coconut milk to thin

Preheat oven to 350°F (180°C). Grease two round 9-inch cake pans with a little oil and dust with cocoa powder, shaking out any excess. Melt chocolate with oil over low heat and set aside. Mix eggs, sugar, milk and vanilla; beat until smooth and creamy. Add melted chocolate and beets and blend until combined.

In a separate bowl, mix the whole wheat flour, almond flour, and baking powder. Then stir chocolate mixture into flour mixture. Pour batter into prepared pans. Bake for 15-17 minutes until top springs back and center is done. Do not overbake! Remove from pans and cool.

FROSTING: Melt chocolate and then mix in sugar, yogurt, milk, and vanilla until smooth. Chill to spreading consistency. Frost between the layers and then spread the rest on the top.

White Chocolate Pavlova Roulade with Berries

This recipe has been my oldest son's "birthday cake" request for the past six years. Don't be scared, assembling it really is a doddle…

[Serves 6-8]

2 bars (7 oz) (200g) white chocolate with coconut (try Lindt's)
or, 200g white chocolate, plus 2 tbsp unsweetened coconut
2 cups (16oz) (450g) plain Greek yogurt
2 tsp vanilla bean paste
white vinegar or lemon juice for wiping bowl and beaters
6 large egg whites, room temperature
1 cup (8 oz) (225g) superfine sugar
½ cup (2 oz) (55g) slivered or flaked almonds
powdered sugar for dusting
2½ cups (12oz) (340g) fresh raspberries, blueberries, or
strawberries

FILLING
Melt white chocolate and stir in coconut. Mix with yogurt and vanilla bean paste and then set aside.

MERINGUE
Wipe a bowl with white vinegar or lemon juice, then add egg whites. Beat with an electric beater until soft peaks form. Gradually add sugar, a large tbsp at a time. Beat until glossy and stiff peaks form.

Line a baking sheet with parchment. Spread meringue about 2 inches thick. Sprinkle with almonds. Bake at 350°F (180°C) for 15-20 minutes until browned and firm, but springy, on top. Remove and cool 5 minutes.

Dust a fresh sheet of parchment with powdered sugar. Then flip the meringue, almond side down, onto this sheet of parchment. Cool to room temperature.

TO ASSEMBLE
Spread the yogurt mixture over the cooled meringue. Top with fruit. Gently lift onto a serving platter, rolling from one narrow end, removing the paper as you roll. Basically, roll the filled meringue off the baking paper onto the serving platter. (It is nearly impossible to lift this dessert in one piece after rolled, so be sure to roll it onto the serving platter.)

Decorate with mint sprigs and fruit. Cut the roll into slices. (This can be made ahead and chilled. Remove from fridge 30 minutes before serving.)

Kings Cake

A French favorite on Epiphany — here, we enjoy it year round!

[Serves 8]

1 large sheet or 2 medium (14 oz) (400g) puff pastry, defrosted but chilled
1 cup (4 oz) (115g) blanched almond flour*
¼ cup (1¼ oz) (35g) coconut sugar
¼ cup (1½ oz) (42g) extra virgin coconut oil
2 large eggs, plus 1 egg beaten for brushing pastry
1 cup (3½ oz) (100g) dark chocolate pieces (70-75%), optional
1 bakeable object for "crowning"

Blend flour, sugar, oil and eggs until thoroughly combined and creamy.

Place half the pastry on baking parchment, covering with second sheet of parchment paper. Roll pastry out to about 11x11. Remove top piece of parchment and brush the outside edges of the pastry with beaten egg.

Spread almond cream to within 1 inch of the edges. Sprinkle chocolate pieces if using over the cream and hide the object. Roll out remaining half of pastry and place on top. Press with a fork to seal edges.

Lightly score top with a knife and chill at least 30 minutes. Brush the top with beaten egg and bake at 350°F (180°C) for 35-40 minutes until golden brown. Cool 10 minutes and then cut into squares.

Crown the lucky one who finds the object in their piece!

To make your own almond flour, simply grind about ¾ cup of whole blanched almonds in a blender to make 1 cup almond flour. Excess almond flour can be stored in the freezer for future use.

Choccie (Avocado!) Mousse

No one will ever guess you snuck so much healthiness into this decadent dessert.

[Serves 4]

4 dates
3½ oz (100g) dark chocolate 70-75%
¼ cup (1½ oz) (42g) extra virgin coconut oil
½ cup (4 fl oz) (125ml) hot water
1 very ripe avocado, pitted and peeled
1 tbsp vanilla bean paste

Soak dates in water for at least 15 minutes in a small bowl. Melt chocolate in a saucepan with the oil. Place dates, water, avocado and vanilla in a blender and blend on high until a smooth paste forms. While machine is running, add dark chocolate mixture and blend until combined. Spoon into decorative glasses or tart shells to serve. Can be enjoyed at room temperature or slightly chilled.

Cranberry Raspberry Cheesecake

Who can resist a cheesecake? Good News!
This one is guilt-free with healthy ingredients and low sugar!

CRUST*

1½ cups whole wheat pastry or sprouted flour
1 tbsp unsulphured molasses
2 tsp ground ginger optional
2½ tbsp honey
3 tbsp extra virgin coconut oil
1 tsp ground cinnamon optional
3 oz (85g) butter, or 2 oz (55g) extra virgin coconut oil, melted

FILLING

2 pkgs (16-oz) (450g) cream cheese
½ cup (2½ oz) (70g) coconut sugar
2 tbsp vanilla bean paste
2 large eggs
2 tsp lemon juice

YOGURT TOPPING

1½ cups (12 oz) (340g) plain Greek yogurt
1 tbsp coconut sugar
1½ tbsp vanilla bean paste

FRUIT TOPPING

1 cup (5 oz) (145g) raspberries
½ cup (2 oz) (55g) dried cranberries
2 tbsp all fruit raspberry jam

By hand or in a food processor, combine flour, molasses, ginger, cinnamon, honey, and 3 tbsp coconut oil. Add melted oil or butter. Press into the bottom and up the sides of a 8-inch springform pan. Set aside.

Blend cream cheese, sugar, vanilla, eggs and juice until smooth. Pour onto crust and bake at 325°F (170°C) for about 50 minutes until set. Turn off the oven and open the door and leave to rest in the oven for 10 minutes.

Meanwhile, mix yogurt with the sugar and vanilla in a bowl.

Heat cranberries and raspberries with the jam and boil for 5 minutes. Pour the cranberry mixture over the cheesecake. Carefully drop dollops of yogurt mixture on top and spread to seal.

Bake at 325°F (170°C) for 10 minutes. Let cool at room temperature. Refrigerate at least 12 hours or overnight. Remove from refrigerator 30 minutes before serving. (This does make a difference in the flavor!)

*GLUTEN FREE CRUST

2 cups (8 oz) (225g) blanched almond flour**
2 tbsp unsulphured molasses
2 tsp ground ginger
1 tsp ground cinnamon
1 tbsp coconut sugar

Blend ingredients until combined. Press into pan.

**To make your own almond flour, simply grind about ¾ cup of whole blanched almonds in a blender to make 1 cup almond flour.*

Flaky Pastry

[Makes 1 crust]

1 cup (4 oz) (115g) whole wheat or sprouted flour
½ tsp sea salt
¼ cup (2 oz) (55g) cold (or frozen) butter
¼ cup (1½ oz) (42g) extra virgin coconut oil, frozen
3 tbsp cold water

Mix flour and salt. Grate frozen butter and oil into the flour mixture. Combine until dough resembles bread crumbs. Mix in cold water until it forms a dough ball. Try not to handle it too much as this will melt the oil and butter and make the pastry tough.

Roll out between 2 layers of unwaxed parchment paper. Chill 20 - 30 minutes. Cut into the shape you need and press into the pan you desire. If you require a pre-baked crust, bake at 375°F (190°C) for about 5-7 minutes until lightly crisp.

Pecan & Pumpkin Pie

Can't decide which pie to make this holiday?
With this easy recipe you can make everyone happy!

[Makes 2 pies]

2 single whole wheat, spelt or gluten free pie crusts, defrosted

PECAN FILLING
2 large organic eggs
¼ cup (1¼ oz) (35g) coconut sugar
⅓ cup (2½ fl oz) (70ml) maple syrup, grade B
1½ cups (6 oz) (175g) pecan pieces

PUMPKIN FILLING
3 large eggs
1 can (15 oz) (425g) organic pumpkin
⅓ cup (2 oz) (55g) coconut sugar
2 tsp each ground cinnamon and ground ginger powder
⅔ cup (5 fl oz) (150ml) unsweetened almond or dairy milk
1½ tsp vanilla paste

Place all pecan filling ingredients except the pecans in a blender and blend until combined. Add pecans. Pour into pie crusts and bake at 375°F (190°C) for 12-15 minutes until set.

Meanwhile, blend all pumpkin filling ingredients. Pour over cooked pecan filling and bake for an additional 25-30 minutes until set. Remove and let stand at least 20 minutes before serving.

Strawberries with Caramel Balsamic Sauce

[Serves 4-6]

CARAMEL
¼ cup (1¼ oz) (35g) coconut sugar
1 tbsp water
3 tbsp unsweetened almond or coconut milk
¼ tsp sea salt

1 lb (450g) fresh whole strawberries with tops on
⅓ cup (3 fl oz) (85ml) balsamic vinegar
½ cup (2 oz) (55g) unshelled pistachios, lightly crushed

Make the caramel by melting the sugar in the water and boil until slightly thickened. Then add the milk and stir until smooth. Stir in salt and set aside.

Boil vinegar in a small saucepan on high for about 4-5 minutes until thickened. (Vinegar should fill no more than 1 inch of the pan.) Be careful not to let it burn. Remove and cool to room temperature.

Place strawberries on a serving plate and drizzle with a little caramel and a little balsamic vinegar. Sprinkle with pistachios.

Summer Fruit with White Chocolate Sauce

[Serves 4-6]

2-3 cups (1-2 lb) (450-900g) fresh strawberries, blueberries, raspberries or any other summer fruit

WHITE CHOCOLATE SAUCE
½ cup (4 fl oz) (125ml) almond or coconut milk
3½ oz (100g) white chocolate

Heat milk until warm, but not boiling. Then melt the chocolate in the warm milk, stirring until it is melted. Drizzle over berries and serve. (The sauce can be made ahead and served cold, room temperature, or reheated.)

Strawberry Ice Cream

[Serves 4]

1 cup (8 oz) (225g) plain Greek yogurt
1 tbsp vanilla bean paste
2 tbsp all fruit strawberry jam
2 cups (8 oz) (225g) frozen strawberries, unsweetened

Place yogurt, vanilla paste, and jam in a blender and blend on high until combined. Add strawberries and continue to blend until thick and smooth. Place in a shallow container in the freezer for one hour. Then beat and refreeze before serving, or process in an ice cream maker. Remove from freezer 20 minutes before serving to soften. (Because it has no added sugar and since strawberries are mostly water, it will freeze very hard!)

Chocolate Sauce to Harden (Chocolate Shell)

My mother loves chocolate sauce that hardens and so do my kids. This is easy to whip up and it uses healthy ingredients. So even though it is a treat, it doesn't wreak health havoc.

[Makes enough for 3-4 sundaes]

3½ oz (100g) 70-75% dark chocolate
2 tbsp extra virgin coconut oil
1 tsp vanilla bean paste (optional)

Melt oil and chocolate on low heat. Stir in vanilla. Cool to room temperature. Pour over ice cream and serve. (Quite wonderful with coconut ice cream!)

[index]